W9-BXT-799

International Standard Book Number: 1-884442-00-5

Printed in the United States of America.

First Printing 1994

Susan:
This is the book
that kept he busy
for such a lengthy
period. How do you
like the format?
Our books could
look like this
or -- if your
creative mind
produces another
one, we'll go with
it.
Bill

William I. Gardner, Ph.D.
University of Wisconsin-Madison

Robert Sovner, M.D.
Tufts Medical School

SELF-INJURIOUS BEHAVIORS

Diagnosis

and

Treatment

A MULTIMODAL FUNCTIONAL APPROACH

VIDA Publishing
Willow Street, Pennsylvania

PREFACE AND ACKNOWLEDGEMENTS

The deinstitutionalization movement has improved the quality of life of those with developmental disabilities. One potential negative effect, however, has been the reduction in routine access to professionals who have expertise in diagnosis and treatment of challenging behavioral and emotional difficulties. In our consultation role to community programs, we have received numerous requests both from professionals (psychologists, physicians, nurses, social workers) with limited knowledge or experience with developmental disabilities and from other concerned persons (case managers, group home parents) for information relating to the causes of and treatments for self-injurious behaviors. Although there is an extensive research literature appearing regularly in a wide array of psychosocial and biomedical journals as well as a steady flow of critical review books and chapters, the practitioner audience typically does not have access to these sources of information or, in some instances, the expertise to translate such information into useful clinical practice.

This Manual has been written for this practitioner audience. Even though some of the materials may be too technical in content for some practitioners, reading of the Manual will insure awareness of current thought and practice. To enhance meaningfulness of the materials, a number of case vignettes are included to illustrate concepts and procedures as these are described. Additionally, an extensive reference and suggested readings listing is provided for further study by the interested reader.

Although this Manual may be used independently of other Manuals in the Series, the reader without background in a biopsychosocial perspective of challenging behaviors or in multimodal behavioral concepts and practices will find the **Behavioral and Emotional Disorders: A Multimodal Functional Approach Treatment Manual** useful as background information.

We wish to express our gratitude and, at the same time, our most sincere apologies to our hundreds of clients with developmental disabilities who present challenging behaviors involving self-injury. Our gratitude is offered to each of you for teaching us to look beyond your self-injurious behaviors and into your array of psychosocial and biological personal features. Only after we began to integrate numerous bits of uniquely personal information did we begin to understand the plethora of influences that contributed to your self-injury. Along with our gratitude for being our teacher, our sincere apologies are offered for our being incompetent on too many occasions in offering the direction that was needed for you to learn other ways of expressing your personal needs. Our hope is that through this Manual other practitioners will have less to apologize for as they will become more skillful in addressing your needs.

William I. Gardner, Ph.D.
Robert Sovner, M.D.

CONTENTS

CONTENTS (continued)

CONTENTS (continued)

CONTENTS (continued)

ONE

Nature of Self-Injurious Behaviors

> *Ms. Irene Brown, a 25-year-old woman with a severe level of mental retardation, is standing in the day room of a small residential facility. She suddenly screams and begins slapping herself in the face. A staff member, sitting across the room and playing a card game with Irene's roommate, states in a loud, firm voice, "Irene, stop that! Control yourself." This only intensifies Irene's repetitive face slapping. The self-injurious behavior stops only after the staff physically intervenes and prompts Irene to join in the card game with her peer.*

Forms of Self-injurious Behaviors

Ms. Brown's self-injurious episodes illustrate one of the most unusual and puzzling behavioral difficulties observed in individuals with mental retardation. It is difficult to understand why she would repeatedly self-inflict pain and risk physical injury. On the surface, it may appear that Ms. Brown actually enjoys such stimulation as she terminates this activity only following staff physical intervention.

Self-injurious behaviors (SIBs) such as Ms. Brown's face-slapping refer to those repetitive and chronic stereotyped acts that either result in direct physical damage or potentially endanger the physical well-being of the person displaying the behaviors. Self-injurious behaviors include such acts as: self-striking (e.g., head banging, face and head slapping); biting various body parts (e.g., biting hands, arms, lips; finger chewing); cutting and burning the skin; pulling, poking, or scratching various body parts (e.g., hair pulling, scratching and picking at wounds, eye poking and gouging, pinching, rectal digging); teeth grinding; and placing objects in body cavities such as ears and nose.

Self-injurious behaviors such as head banging may take many forms including hitting one's head on the floor, wall, chair or other hard objects. In another individual, or even with the same person, self-injury may take such forms as hitting one's chin with his or her fist or banging one's head against the knees. Among those who exhibit SIBs, head banging, self-biting, self-striking (e.g., slapping, punching), and scratching occur with greatest frequency. It is estimated that over 50% of those engaging in SIBs exhibit more than one form, e.g., head banging, self-biting, and self-pinching.

Two additional infrequently occurring forms of self-injury observed among those with developmental disabilities that can result in serious medical problems are those of aerophagia and polydipsia. **Aerophagia** refers to excessive or prolonged air swallowing resulting in abdominal distention, excessive flatus, and frequent belching. Chronic aerophagia may produce abnormal structural changes in the gastrointestinal system and compression of the diaphragm. **Psychogenic polydipsia** refers to water drinking that greatly exceeds physiological requirements. The excessive fluid intake may produce such signs of water intoxication as vomiting, agitation, incoordination, seizures, and coma. Although polydipsia-induced water intoxication occurs primarily in persons with psychiatric diagnoses of schizophrenia or psychotic depression, this form of self-injury does occur occasionally among those with developmental disabilities with accompanying mental disorder diagnoses such as schizophrenia and autistic disorder.

Some authorities consider repeated vomiting and the reingestion of food (rumination) and the consumption of nonedible substances (i.e., pica--eating items such as cigarette butts or twigs, coprophagy-eating feces) to be forms of SIBs. These disorders, however, will be described in a separate **Diagnosis and Treatment Manual** because of their unique features.

Individual Differences in Type and Severity

Marked individual differences are evident in the type, severity, frequency and duration of self-injurious episodes. In some persons, self-injurious behaviors may be stereotyped and occur hundreds of times and in numerous situations throughout the day as illustrated by an individual who repetitively bangs his fist against his head for extended periods. Other forms of SIBs may be relatively nonrepetitious (e.g., eye gouging and rectal digging) and may occur only in certain situations or at certain times and thus be under the influence of highly specific conditions. In other instances, SIBs may be highly variable in occurrence, often unpredictable, and prone to occur across varying situations.

Some individuals may display only a single SIB such as hand biting, head banging, cutting or burning the skin, or face and head slapping; others, as noted, may display multiple forms of SIBs. The majority of individuals who engage in self-injury demonstrate other stereotyped behaviors such as repetitive screaming and body rocking. In addition, in some persons SIBs occur in a sequence or chain of other aberrant behaviors as illustrated by Mr. Stevens:

Mr. John Stevens, a 35-year-old man with moderate impairment in cognitive and adaptive behavior features, currently resides in a special treatment unit of a regional mental health facility. He has a lengthy history of severe episodes of agitated/disruptive behaviors that include complaining, yelling, threats of violence toward self and others, disrobing in public places, physical aggression toward staff and peers, property damage and destruction, and self-injury. The self-injurious acts, consisting of slapping and punching himself in the face and head, head banging against furniture and walls, and scratching his face, most typically occur as the last behavior in a sequence of behaviors. These SIBs can be managed through successful intervention earlier in the behavioral chain of events.

Comorbidity: Risk Factors

Although SIBs may occur among individuals with mild and moderate levels of mental retardation, the greatest frequency and severity is observed among individuals with severe and profound mental retardation, communication deficits, especially those reflecting receptive skills more advanced than expressive skills, sensory disabilities, lengthy histories of institutional living, and with diagnoses of brain-injury, seizure disorders, pervasive developmental disorder with associated severe social impairment, and specific medical disorders such as Lesch-Nyhan syndrome. In addition, some forms of SIBs may coexist with various mental disorders such as borderline personality disorders, psychoses, major depression, autistic disorder, and stereotypy/habit disorder. Such acts of self-injury as cutting and burning the skin and sticking objects under the skin, when observed, occur typically among those with mild cognitive impairments and accompanying psychiatric impairments.

While few of these disorders or conditions would be viewed as **primary** causes of the SIBs, these may be viewed as **risk** or **predisposing** factors that increase the likelihood of the initiation and recurrence of SIBs when other instigating conditions are present. More detailed descriptions of biomedical risk factors are included in Chapter 3.

Prevalence of Self-Injurious Behaviors

Although reported to occur in all age groups, a higher prevalence of SIBs is observed in those below 30 years of age. Typically, the lower the person's IQ level, the more frequent, severe, and treatment resistant the SIBs are likely to be. Various studies have reported rates ranging from 8% to over 20% of individuals with mental retardation living in institutions and from 2% to 11% of those living outside of institutions. Females, especially among children, have a lower rate of occurrence than males.

Prevalent Interventions

Various studies report that 30-50% of individuals with SIBs receive psychotropic medication to manage these problem behaviors. In fact, recent data indicate that, next to aggression and related agitated/ disruptive behaviors, SIBs are the most commonly recorded behaviors of persons receiving psychotropic medication. This widespread use of psychotropic medication is present even though the general treatment efficacy of these drugs for SIBs has not been established. At this time there is no successful pharmacotherapy for SIBs. As discussed in later sections, when SIBs reflect the effects of various physical and mental illnesses or disorders such as depression or anxiety, treatment of these underlying disorders may result in reduction in SIBs. In addition, evolving theoretical biochemical models are beginning to offer possible pharmacological agents that may prove valuable in selective cases of chronic SIBs.

Although various behavioral interventions have demonstrated efficacy in selected instances, these are not available to most persons with chronic SIBs due to the professional effort and time required for adequate implementation. As a consequence of the current knowledge base and limited availabiity of resources, severe SIBs typically are managed by use of medication and such protective devices as helmets and mechanical restraining devices such as cuffs, straps, splints, and vests.

Significance of Self-Injurious Behaviors

Self-injurious behaviors are significant not only because the person is placed in serious jeopardy of physical harm (e.g., tissue damage, amputation, fractures, loss of vision) but also because frequent and intense episodes of self-injurious acts interfere with efforts at providing positive social and educational experiences for the person. As a result, development of the person's social, emotional, intellectual, and adaptive behavior characteristics are impeded. In addition, the physical and chemical procedures frequently used to manage and protect the person may interfere significantly with habilitative program efforts. The cost of care and treatment of severe cases requiring residential placement can run as high as $100,000 per year. Finally, the prolonged use of various physical and/or chemical restraints as means of managing or minimizing the frequency and intensity of SIBs may result in permanent physical and/or neurological damage to the person.

Developmental Nature of SIBs

Specific biomedical or psychosocial conditions seldom result directly in SIB's. An exception may be seen in cases of involuntary self-injurious movements associated with seizure disorders. Other possible exceptions reflecting biomedical conditions are discussed in Chapter 3. Chronic self-injury in most instances may be viewed as representing learned behaviors that have been shaped and strengthened gradually by contingent reinforcing consequences.

Initial Onset

The reinforcement view of the development of chronic self-injury offers two hypotheses relating to the initial onset of self-injury, viz., the **overarousal hypothesis** and the **homeostatic hypothesis**.

Overarousal Hypothesis

In this learning model of initial onset, SIBs may reflect a rage, fear, or overarousal reaction to various painful or stressful circumstances. The SIBs represent an attempt to reduce the high arousal level arising from the fear, anxiety, or other sources of discomfort such as an inner ear infection. The SIBs may produce reduction or termination of the arousal-inducing condition as well as associated social feedback and thereby are reinforced by these consequences. This reinforcement adds to the likelihood of recurrence of SIBs at a future time under similar stimulus conditions. In this manner, the self-injury becomes a coping (functional) behavior.

Homeostatic Hypothesis

The second learning view of the conditions giving rise to the initial onset of self-injury reflects a homeostatic theory. From this perspective, stereotypy occurs in understimulating environments as a means of regulating a desired level of arousal. The intensity of the stereotypic movements may be shaped inadvertently by contingent social feedback to the point that the behavior becomes self-injurious. The person gradually learns that the more intense forms (SIBs) of the rhythmic movements most reliably produce reinforcing social feedback.

Maintenance of SIBs

Following initial onset, any specific future experience may exert only a minute influence on the development, maintenance, and current presentation of self-injury as a functional response in the person's behavioral repertoire. However, the gradual cumulative effect of 50, 100, 500 or more learning experiences in which SIBs serve one or more adaptive functions for the person may result in self-injurious responses that become habitual and highly resistant to change.

Multimodal Functional Approach: Overview

As is evident, self-injury is a complex phenomenon and, as documented more fully in the chapters to follow, represents the end result of a variety of biomedical and psychosocial influences. As with any maladaptive behavior, self-injury may serve a variety of functions for an individual. A person's habitual SIBs may reflect, as illustrations, attempts to (a) obtain social feedback, (b) escape from or even avoid specific demands or other aversive conditions, (c) modulate unpleasant mood states (e.g., anxiety, dysphoria), and (d) control physical pain.

Although a multiplicity of factors may contribute to SIBs, all too frequently, as noted, prevalent biomedical and psychosocial interventions reflect either **management** and **control** procedures or those designed to suppress the behavior independently of knowledge of the conditions influencing its occurrence. As a result, only minimum, if any, long-term reduction in the person's inclination to engage in SIBs is realized. It is not unusual for the practitioner to accept self-injury as a chronic condition that seemingly is treatment resistant.

This Treatment Manual, in contrast to these prevalent practices, emphasizes the value of interventions that address directly the functionality of the self-injury, that is, are designed to modify those conditions involved in the instigation and habitual recurrence of these aberrant behaviors. To reflect the multiple and complex factors involved in the instigation and maintenance of self-injury, a **Multimodal Functional Diagnostic and Intervention Model** is offered to guide the practitioner in developing initial diagnostic formulations and in translating these, when relevant, into an integrated set of biomedical and psychosocial interventions.

The Multimodal Functional Model reflects a **biopsychosocial** view of SIBs in emphasizing that these behaviors currently represent the joint influences of a person with psychological and biomedical characteristics as he/she interacts with physical and psychosocial environments. The initial step in devising an intervention program consists of the development of a set of interrelated diagnostic and treatment formulations reflecting biomedical, psychological, and social influences. Such formulations are necessary as self-injury is best viewed as a "final common pathway" reflecting an individual's adaptation to environmental demands and physical discomfort as well as to disturbances in neurochemical and physiological function.

In view of the potential for multiple factors to contribute to the functionality of SIBs, there can be no single biomedical or psychosocial intervention. Self-injury associated with rage attacks, for example, may respond favorably to beta adrenergic receptor blocker therapy (e.g., propranolol) whereas SIBs associated with manic irritability will not. Self-injury that is motivated by an attempt to escape from an aversive task demand will not respond to an intervention tactic of increased staff attention. In sum, interventions must address the person-specific complex of instigating and maintaining conditions if enduring change in a person's SIBs is to be realized.

Functional Diagnostic Formulations: Overview

In developing an understanding of a person's SIBs as a means of selecting person-specific interventions, a set of diagnostic formulations evolve from the following three-step process:

Step 1 The primary diagnostic task initially faced by the practitioner is that of identifying the current **external** (e.g., specific task demands, reduced social attention) and **internal** (e.g., anxiety, premenstrual pain, anger, organically-based overarousal) stimulus conditions of a biomedical, psychological, or socioenvironmental nature that contribute directly to the **instigation** of the SIBs. These instigating conditions, as described in Chapter 2, are viewed as serving either a primary or secondary function.

Step 2 Following this initial step of placing the SIBs in a context of instigating stimulus conditions, hypotheses are developed regarding the **functionality** of the SIBs. Given the instigating stimulus conditions, assessment seeks to determine the purposes or functions being served by the SIBs (e.g., terminate aversive demands, modulate pain, decrease unpleasant internal arousal, insure physical contact and other social feedback).

Step 3 As a final step in the diagnostic formulation process, these observations are combined with those describing other relevant **personal** features of a psychological (e.g., anger management, communication, or coping skills deficits) and biomedical (e.g., sensory, neurological, or biochemical impairments or abnormalities) nature along with **socioenvironmental or ecological** features (e.g., limited opportunity for social interaction, restrictions in type and frequency of structured program activities) that may be of significance in understanding a person's SIBs. These are viewed, as described in Chapter 2, as tertiary or vulnerability influences.

Functional Intervention Formulations: Overview

| Step 4 | These hunches about primary and secondary instigating conditions, the functionality of the SIBs, and the tertiary vulnerability factors form the basis for formulation of diagnostically-based interventions addressing each of the presumed contributing influences. Major program efforts are focused on (a) removing or minimizing biomedical and psychosocial factors presumed to be involved in instigating and maintaining the SIBs, (b) teaching prosocial coping skills as well as increasing the personal motivation to use these newly acquired skills as adaptive functional replacements for the maladaptive symptoms, and (c) on reducing or eliminating impoverished socioenvironmental conditions and biomedical abnormalities. A skill enhancement program focus is especially pertinent for persons with highly impoverished repertoires of coping behaviors. In this personal context, SIBs may represent highly effective and efficient functional behaviors and must be replaced by equally effective and efficient functionally equivalent coping skills if the SIBs are to be minimized or eliminated.

The content and process of devising these diagnostic-intervention formulations along with related concepts of the Multimodal Functional Model are provided elaboration in Chapter 2.

SUMMARY

Self-injurious behaviors occur with greatest frequency among persons with severe and profound mental retardation, pronounced communication deficits, sensory disabilities, mental disorders, brain injury, seizure disorders, pervasive developmental disabilities, and with specific medical disorders such as Lesch-Nyhan syndrome. Conditions associated with initial onset may differ from those involved in influencing the persistent occurrence of self-injury. Prevalent interventions include those involving psychotropic medication and management with the use of various protective devices and mechanical restraints. An alternative Multimodal Functional approach to diagnosis and intervention of self-injury is represented in this Treatment Manual. Chapter 2 introduces the central assessment and intervention concepts associated with this approach.

TWO

Multimodal Functional Model: Assessment and Intervention Concepts

Introduction

A functional diagnostic model that guides the development of an intervention program for self-injury was introduced in Chapter 1. This diagnostic model, based on the biopsychosocial perspective described earlier, includes assessment of those variables involved in the **instigation** of problem behaviors as well as those contributing to the **acquisition** and **persistent recurrence** of these.   Figure 2.1 provides a depiction of the multiple variables evaluated in this functional diagnostic activity.

This diagnostic assessment seeks to identify the multiple biomedical, psychological, and environmental variables that currently influence a person's SIBs. As there is no single or simple psychological or biomedical mechanism that underlies this problem, and as most problem behaviors such as self-injury are interpersonal and viewed and treated in the context of social interactions, a functional diagnostic assessment includes evaluation of the interpersonal/environmental context of the person's difficulties as well as the person's unique biomedical and psychological structures and dynamics.

The diagnostic assessment is **person-specific**. In illustration, one person may impulsively engage in SIBs when angry or overly anxious, while another individual's SIBs may be more deliberate and goal-directed. The diagnostic-intervention formulations obviously would differ for these persons.

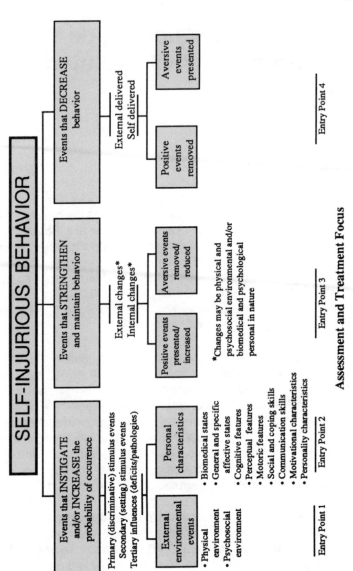

Figure 2.1 Multimodal Functional Diagnostic and Treatment Model

As depicted in Figure 2.2, some of the psychological characteristics included in Figure 2.1 such as social and coping skills, communication skills, motivational features, and personality characteristics, by
their absence or low strength, may increase the likelihood of SIBs in
those persons inclined to use self-injury to cope with external or internal
instigating conditions. No functionally equivalent alternative behaviors
may be present in the person's repertoire or, if present, may not be as
effective or efficient as the SIBs. Thus, when attempting to understand
and program for a person's current problems involving self-injury,
knowledge of these **tertiary** conditions (deficit areas) guides the clinician in simultaneously pinpointing the specific functionally equivalent
coping skills and related cognitive, emotional, and motivational supports that will be needed for continued successful social and interpersonal functioning following termination of an intervention program.

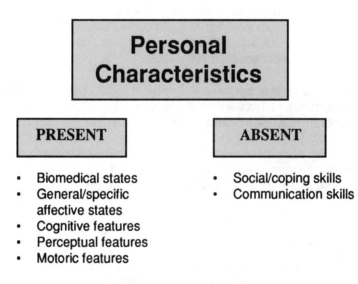

Figure 2.2 Personal Characteristics Influencing SIBs

Objectives of Functional Diagnostics

The objectives of a functional diagnostic assessment, as noted earlier, are threefold:

• to identify the various primary and secondary internal biomedical and psychological conditions and external physical and psychosocial conditions under which SIBs are likely to occur,

• to identify the functions served by the SIBs (i.e., What do the SIBs currently contribute to the person?), and

• to identify various tertiary personal (biomedical and psychological) and socioenvironmental features that contribute indirectly both to the instigation and continuation of the SIBs.

An understanding of person-specific biomedical, psychological, and socioenvironmental influences provides the foundation for an intervention program that holds promise of producing durable therapeutic gains.

To illustrate the value of an individualized diagnostic assessment and the central assumption that recurring SIBs are **functional** in that these serve some purpose(s), consider Janice Harbor:

The recurring self-injurious behaviors of Ms. Harbor, a young adult with severe mental retardation who resides in a group home, may serve a number of different purposes or functions.   The behaviors may, as examples:

- *produce valued social attention from group home parents and/or peers,*

- *result in the removal of undesired requests or directives,*

- *result in reduction of an internal state of emotional arousal such as anger or anxiety,*

- *provide valuable sensory stimulation,*

- *produce signs of distress in others, and/or*

- *result in a sense of influence or control over others.*

Further, the behaviors may be most likely to occur at certain times such as during a day or two following weekend visits from parents. An effective individualized intervention program can not be developed until assessment of the unique set of factors contributing to the self-injury is completed. These assessment data form the basis for the intervention experiences.

Instigating Conditions: Environmental

The initial focus of assessment is the identification of antecedent conditions that, individually or in combination, instigate self-injury. As depicted in Figure 2.1, these include external environmental conditions. These environmental antecedent conditions may serve a **primary instigating** or a **secondary instigating** function. Additionally, other environmental features may serve as **tertiary** influences. In illustration of the latter, a highly impoverished physical and/or social environment that provides limited opportunity for sensory or social stimulation may contribute to a person's SIBs due to the restricted availability of other ways of obtaining valued feedback. Events that occur in the external environment are described initially and followed by consideration of various client characteristics.

Primary Instigating Events

SIBs currently in a person's repertoire do not occur randomly or haphazardly. Rather, SIBs as only one component of the person's total array of appropriate and inappropriate behaviors occur at certain times, in specific places, and under certain conditions. These external stimuli may include both **physical** (e.g., noise level) and **social** (e.g., someone staring) events. Specific stimulus events or cues begin to gain influence over the occurrence of SIBs by being associated repeatedly with specific and predictable reinforcing consequences produced by these acts. As a result of this behavior-consequence relationship, SIBs, instead of other behaviors in the person's repertoire, are more likely to occur in the presence of specific physical stimuli, specific people, at certain times and places, or following other specific types of cues such as tone of voice with which a directive is presented, or the difficulty level of a task. Also, these behaviors are unlikely to occur in situations in which reinforcement has not occurred or in which contingent negative consequences have been present. Again, SIBs become specific to various preceding conditions as these signal the occurrence of specific consequences associated with the self-injury.

These controlling or instigating cues that signal the time, place, and conditions under which specific behaviors (e.g., head banging) are likely to result in specific consequences (e.g., removal of boring tasks, staff attention) are called **primary** instigating conditions or **discriminative** events. In illustration:

> *Donald Hines may engage in SIBs whenever his father reminds him to complete an assigned responsibility such as cleaning his dishes following a meal. The father's verbal reminder is a cue (i.e., discriminative stimulus or event) for the self-injury. Such behavior in the past apparently has resulted in consequences that Donald found valuable (e.g., creating distress in father,*

> sibling attention) or has removed something that he
> disliked (e.g., being excused from cleaning dishes, a
> task which he finds distasteful).

As a second example:

> *Jean Jones, a 12-year-old with severe mental retarda-*
> *tion, minimal speech, and numerous challenging be-*
> *haviors, may be observed to hit her head with her fist*
> *under various conditions such as a sudden increase in*
> *noise level, a peer taking one of her possessions, or*
> *following periods of being ignored by group-home staff.*
> *These conditions or events may prompt the SIBs*
> *because these acts previously have resulted in staff*
> *intervention in reducing the noise level, returning her*
> *possessions, and/or in providing individual social at-*
> *tention. This observation emphasizes that the SIBs*
> *may serve a variety of functions for the child.*

An initial focus of assessment thus involves identification of
interpersonal and other potential influences of the external psychosocial and physical environments that instigate the self-injury (see Entry
Point 1 of Figure 2.1). These stimulus conditions are viewed as **primary**
instigating events as the SIBs only occur when these conditions are
present. As illustrated above, the SIBs of a person may be instigated
by the presentation of more than one primary discriminative condition.
Information is obtained relative to these specific instigating events such
as a work supervisor's reprimands for substandard work performance,
the termination or reduction in frequency of staff attention, directives
from a specific staff, or taunts of a peer as well as other sources of
environmental stimulation such as high noise level, overcrowding, or
agitated peer models that may result in aberrant reactions. As
illustrated in Chapter 6, knowledge of the relative influence of various
primary instigating conditions and the increased influence when combined with specific secondary setting events is of significant value in

devising intervention programs and in setting program priorities.

The physical and social events triggering or instigating self-injurious behaviors obviously are **person specific** and can best be identified through systematic direct observation of an individual in those particular situations in which the behaviors occur. That assessment must be individualized has been emphasized by studies that reveal wide individual differences among persons with mental retardation in the types of antecedent conditions that serve to instigate self-injury. Conditions such as social disapproval, adult demands, and reduced social attention result in varying effects on the likelihood of SIBs of different persons. (See Chapter 6 for discussion of alternatives to direct observation as assessment procedures including checklists, interviews with knowledgeable family, caregiver or program staff, and exposure of the person to analogue conditions.)

Secondary Instigating Events

In addition to these immediately preceding discriminative events, other stimulus conditions may influence the person to engage in SIBs. These types of stimulus conditions are called **secondary** instigating conditions or **setting** events as their presence or absence provides a "set," activation, or inclination for the person to behave in a particular manner when exposed to various primary discriminative stimuli. These setting events may represent historical, durational, and covert (physical, affective, cognitive, perceptual) conditions. Description of **historical** and **durational** events is followed in the next section on client characteristics by discussion of **covert** setting events.

Behavioral History

A person's **behavioral history** (temporally distant experiences wholly separate in space and time from current stimulus conditions) may set the person to behave in either a positive or negative manner. For example:

> *An adolescent who had been fighting with a peer on the school bus may be more prone after arriving in the classroom to engage in SIBs when confronted with such specific discriminative events as being teased by peers or provided corrective feedback by staff.*

In a similar manner, a prior positive experience may facilitate the occurrence of positive behaviors when later presented with specific discriminative events.

> *This is illustrated by an adult with severe mental retardation who returns from a shopping trip with a favorite staff member. Even though he typically displays SIBs when staff directives are provided, as a result of this trip he may be unusually cooperative later in the day in following specific requests of his group home parents. The positive experience occurring hours before continues to influence the person to behave in a positive manner, even in the presence of current events that typically result in self-injurious behaviors.*

The effects of these historical setting events thus may either **facilitate** or **inhibit** the occurrence of existing stimulus-response functions that follow the setting events. To emphasize, some setting events may occur well before but still facilitate, or inhibit, the occurrence of later stimulus-response relationships involving self-injury.

Durational Events

In addition to the earlier occurring events that "set" the person to behave in a specific manner, **durational events** such as the mere presence of certain people or conditions (e.g., female staff member, reinforcement contingency, specific production requirement in the work setting, noisy or crowded environment, infrequent social attention) that are aversive to a person may influence his or her reactions to other current stimulus conditions. Other durational events that may produce setting states of arousal include general environmental conditions such as amount of space, staff/client ratio, time of day, presence or absence of leisure materials, level of difficulty of classroom or workshop tasks, and behaviors of staff or peers. In illustration:

> *When Tim Smith, a group home staff member, is present in the home, Jane Hanks typically is cooperative with other staff members in completing her chores. However, when Tim is off duty and replaced by another staff member, Jane is likely to refuse to complete her daily responsibilities and to display SIBs if directed repeatedly to complete these activities.*

Summary

Identification of externally occurring primary (discriminative) and secondary (setting) events that serve to instigate or influence the occurrence of specific behaviors is of value as such information offers a possible means of influencing a person's self-injury. If, for example, a person is likely to engage in SIBs under the combined conditions of being teased by peers when exposed to noisy conditions in his living areas, it may be possible to decrease the self-injury by managing the secondary setting condition of noise level. Or, if excessive arguments among peers result in an innocent bystander becoming increasingly agitated and engaging in SIBs when directed to leave the program area, this self-injury may be managed by reducing or terminating disruptive arguments among peers. Additionally in both instances, a treatment strategy could be followed in teaching the persons specific skills of coping with the stimulus complex in ways other than through self-injury.

Instigating Conditions: Psychological Characteristics

A number of client characteristics of a psychological nature also have been implicated as influential in producing or contributing to the occurrence of self-injurious behaviors (see Entry Point 2 of Figure 2.1). These include conditions that, in isolation or in combination with external events or other internal biomedically-based conditions, instigate or increase the likelihood of these reactions. Thus, psychological features of the person may serve as **primary discriminative** and as **secondary setting** stimulus conditions. These psychological characteristics include both transitory and more enduring **affective states** such as anger, depression, anxiety, chronic sadness; **cognitive variables** such as provocative covert ruminations and paranoid ideation; **perceptual features** such as auditory and visual hallucinations; and **motoric features** such as the overactivity associated with mania or attention-deficit hyperactivity disorder.

In most instances, these psychological characteristics serve as secondary or setting event influences and result in SIBs only in combination with specific primary instigating conditions. This function is illustrated by Ms. Claire Irvine.

> *Ms. Claire Irvine may be most likely to engage in SIBs when criticized by a peer only when in a "bad mood." She may seldom demonstrate self-injury, even under peer provocation, when in a "good mood." Or she may be disappointed that her parents did not come for a visit at the expected time. The resulting emotional state of irritability may "set" her to respond with self-injury to minor sources of aggravation that typically would be ignored by her.*

In some cases, these psychological characteristics may serve a primary instigating function and independently produce SIBs. A person with severe distress associated with a high anxiety level and no functional communication skills for use in soliciting assistance from others may repeatedly engage in face and head slapping in an attempt to reduce the level of distress.

Also of interest are those **deficit** skill areas or **tertiary** influences depicted in Figure 2.2, such as communication, social, and related problem solving and coping skills that, due to their low strength or absence, contribute to the **vulnerability** of the person to engage in inappropriate responding, including self-injury, under various conditions of provocation. As suggested earlier, in the context of an impoverished repertoire of alternative functional skills, the SIBs may be the most effective and efficient means of coping with various primary and secondary sources of provocation. This correlation between skill deficits and SIBs suggests a program focus on teaching alternative functional coping skills as a means of reducing the person's vulnerability.

Finally, trait or **personality** variables and **motivational** features of the person may contribute to self-injury. A person with profound mental retardation, in illustration of the latter, may have a generalized low threshold for tolerating changes and thus be prone to self-injury and other agitated/disruptive outbursts under frequent unplanned disruptions in his daily routine. Knowledge of events that reflect the motivational inclinations including those that serve as positive reinforcers (e.g., adult approval, peer acceptance, exerting control over others, aggravating others), and the variety and relative effects of aversive events that influence the person's behaviors (e.g., rejection by peers, difficult task demands, adult reprimand) is of value in identifying potential instigating and tertiary influences and for development of related interventions.

In sum, such psychological characteristics as excessive negative emotional arousal, paranoid ideation, or generalized irritability may **by their presence** serve as primary or secondary conditions and thus instigate or increase the likelihood of aberrant responding. Other tertiary variables, such as communication skills and motivation to please others, **by their absence or low strength,** may render the person more vulnerable to problem responding under specific conditions of provocation.

Instigating Conditions: Biomedical Factors

Even though recurring patterns of SIBs do reflect the influence of various psychological features of the person, these also reflect the influences of a range of individually unique biomedical states and conditions such as fatigue, seizure activity, drug effects, chronic pain, overarousal and irritability associated with neurological impairment, mental disorders, and premenstrual discomfort. In some instances, various biomedical factors may represent the **primary** or **discriminative stimulus** factor influencing SIBs; in others, biomedical influences may be **secondary** and serve as a **setting** condition to increase the frequency, intensity, and duration of previously learned and currently existing problems of SIBs only when combined with other primary discriminative conditions. These primary and secondary effects are discussed and illustrated in the following sections.

Other abnormal biomedical features may serve as **tertiary** influences through limiting a person's response equipment—his or her sensory, motoric, and/or neurological connecting systems—and thus interfere with or reduce normal response potential. These abnormalities may indirectly contribute to aberrant responding.

Chronic Versus Transitional Influences

Some biomedical factors represent **trait** or **chronic** effects, as seen in hormonal or enzyme deficiencies, neurotransmitter abnormalities, a structurally damaged brain, chronic pain, or seizure activity. Persons treated with psychoactive drugs over extended periods of time may develop such adverse behavioral side-effects as agitation, overarousal, irritability, anxiety, overactivity, behavioral disinhibition, and symptoms of depression such as emotional and behavioral withdrawal. In the case of sensory and muscular disabilities, the person may be limited in the types and intensities of stimuli to which he or she may be receptive and to the types of responses which he or she can make. In sum, the person's current behavior, including self-injury, will reflect the influence of these individually unique biomedical states or conditions. Biomedical intervention to reduce the person's organically-based chronic overarousal, in illustration, may be required over an extended period of time due to the chronic nature of the organic condition.

Other biomedical states, such as fatigue, hunger, toothache, constipation, a brief low blood sugar level, those associated with changes in type or dose of psychoactive medication, or as illustrated below by Deborah, premenstrual discomfort and irritability, represent **temporary, transitional**, or **state** conditions. Although temporary, these may nonetheless influence how a person will behave at specific times and situations. Any of these states may exert significant influence on the manner in which the person will respond to various external events such as overall noise or activity levels, a directive from a teacher, or a taunt from a peer. Deborah Woodward provides illustration of these biomedical influences:

Ms. Woodward is a 26-year-old woman with an autistic disorder. She has a recent history of infrequent but intense agitated/disruptive outbursts during which she would bite peers, staff, or herself, push, pull hair, pinch, scratch, scream and refuse to participate in various program activities which typically she finds enjoyable. Deborah also has periods of days and even weeks without any problem behaviors.

Evaluation of the episodic nature of these behavioral outbursts suggest a high correlation between an increased frequency and intensity of the disruptive behaviors and Deborah's menses. Medical treatment combined with a reduction of program requirements during her periods of increased irritability resulted in a significant reduction in her agitated/disruptive episodes.

Modification of these internal instigating conditions by biomedical interventions may produce an immediate effect on the frequency and severity of self-injury. Following remission of these transitional biomedical conditions, the intervention can be discontinued.

Primary Effects of Biomedical Factors

The type and relative influence of biomedical factors on self-injury will vary. In some instances, as noted, current biomedical conditions may represent a **primary** or **discriminative event** influence on specific patterns of SIBs. Mental disorders such as schizophrenia, major depression, or bipolar disorder represent examples of these. Frequency and severity of SIBs may increase noticeably upon occurrence of these mental disorders or may, in some instances, only occur in conjunction with a psychiatric condition such as a major mood disorder. In these instances, the SIBs may be instigated by and represent attempts to modulate the internal psychological distress. Treatment of the presumed biochemical abnormalities associated with these disorders with psychopharmacological agents, and thereby reducing/removing the psychological distress, holds promise of reducing the presenting self-injurious episodes by eliminating the primary instigating condition.

To emphasize, client characteristics reflecting physical and psychiatric biomedical internal conditions (Figure 2.1, Entry 2) may serve as primary discriminative stimulus events independent of any specific external provocation, and thus cue or instigate overt behavior. The discriminative influence of internal biomedical conditions on overt behaviors is further illustrated by Anthony Barnes:

> *Anthony, a child with profound developmental delays and minimal communication skills, attends a developmental education day program. While sitting alone at his desk, he suddenly begins slapping his ear with his open hand as he screams loudly. On examination by the school nurse, it is discovered that Anthony has an ear infection. The pain caused by the infection apparently served as a discriminative event for the self-injurious behavior.*

The tertiary influence of Anthony's communication skill deficits on occurrence of the SIBs is apparent.

Secondary Effects of Biomedical Factors

In most instances of self-injury, biomedical factors will represent a **secondary** or **setting event** influence on a person's SIBs. Increased irritability related to a seizure medication or to central nervous system damage may render a person generally more prone to self-injurious episodes when confronted with specific environmental or interpersonal stressors. Reduction of this organically-based over-arousal by medication or medication change may decrease the frequency, duration, and intensity of episodes of SIBs on exposure to primary instigating conditions. In addition, this reduction would render the person more available to benefit from, in illustration, such psychosocial interventions as a coping skills training program involving gradual exposure to the external stressors while teaching alternative relaxation or other competing responses.

As an additional example of a secondary or setting event biomedical condition:

> *Mr. Douglas Carter, a person with profound mental retardation and an arousal state characterized by generalized irritability or restlessness (physiological setting event), frequently engages in SIBs when exposed to minor sources of external provocation (discriminative events). Under the assumption that the generalized irritability and restlessness is organically-based, Mr. Carter's threshold for aberrant responding may be raised by providing drug therapy that addresses the neuropsychiatric conditions producing the overarousal. A reduction in irritability and restlessness may result in more appropriate responding to externally-presented events. In this instance, the self-injury is reduced by managing the setting event component of the stimulus complex involved in its instigation.*

Biomedical and Psychological Interactions

In some cases, self-injury that appears to be the direct result of physical factors actually may be influenced by psychosocial factors. The severe self-injurious behaviors of persons with Lesch-Nyhan syndrome, although highly correlated with the associated medical conditions and presumed to be directly instigated and maintained by biomedical factors, may also be influenced by the social feedback produced by the SIBs. Rick Ford illustrates this influence.

Since placement ten years ago in a private residential facility, 30-year-old Mr. Ford has required physical restraint to control his self-mutilation. It had been assumed that his self-injury, when released from restraints, was caused by his Lesch-Nyhan syndrome. A recent behavioral program, however, has demonstrated that a significant number of his attempted and successful SIBs have specific communicative components. Teaching Rick alternative forms of communication that provide him control over when his restraints should be removed has resulted in a significant decrease in SIBs and a concomitant increase in periods without restraints.

Covert Instigating Conditions: Summary

Internal sources of stimulation reflecting psychological and biomedical events represent potential primary instigating conditions as well as a **third class of setting events**. These **covert** setting events increase or decrease the likelihood that self-injury will occur in the presence of various other specific primary discriminative events. As these internal setting events may either facilitate or inhibit what a person does under other specific stimulus conditions, these represent potential targets for therapeutic intervention as previously illustrated. As other examples:

Disruptive behaviors including self-injury during a structured academic class may be reduced in a group of overly anxious students by using the initial five minutes of the class period as a rest or relaxation period

> *designed to create an emotional state supportive of appropriate classroom behavior. Or, if a person is prone to self-injury when in a state of emotional irritability and to behave appropriately when in a positive emotional state, initial efforts at changing the person's negative affective state to a positive one should result in a set to respond cooperatively to specific requests made of him.*

Instigating Conditions: Stimulus Complex

When assessing external and internal events that may serve to instigate SIBs, it is highly unusual to identify primary discriminative events reflecting physical or psychological conditions in the presence of which these behaviors always occur. In most instances, a **stimulus complex** sets the occasion for maladaptive reactions. This complex frequently involves both primary and secondary influences representing internal as well as external stimulus conditions. Additionally, these instigating conditions vary in the probability of producing the SIBs. In illustration, an adolescent with severe mental retardation who is highly prone to engage in SIBs under conditions of negative social provocation may behave appropriately on some occasions when in a state of positive emotional arousal even when taunted by a peer. When aroused negatively (e.g., being angry or irritable over prolonged verbal rumination concerning a previous reprimand by a teacher), the same adolescent under the same external provocation is most likely to engage in self-injury. This diagnostic information would suggest that the critical variable requiring treatment is the person's lack of coping skills under the dual conditions of negative emotional arousal and peer teasing.

Of importance is the observation that historical, durational, or covert setting events are not constant across persons, or even for the same person across time and situations. In illustration, the mere presence of a physically large male staff member (as a durational setting event) may serve to inhibit self-injury in a client who is likely to head-bang when reprimanded by other staff. However, this same large male staff member may have no such "setting" effect on another person under the same reprimand stimulus conditions. These setting events thus must be empirically and individually defined and identified.

Finally, tertiary factors representing deficits or pathologies of biomedical, psychological, and socioenvironmental conditions and features contribute indirectly to the occurrence of SIBs. These require identification and translation into diagnostic hypotheses relating to the specific role assumed in each individual case. These tertiary factors are discussed further in the sections to follow.

Consequences of Behavior

The final set of variables evaluated are those psychosocial and biomedical factors that may contribute to the functionality of the problem behaviors (see Entry Point 3 of Figure 2.1). Consequences assessed include both positive events gained following the occurrence of self-injury (i.e., positive reinforcement) as well as aversive conditions removed, reduced, or postponed following these actions (i.e., negative reinforcement). As discussed in Chapter 4, SIBs may become functional in producing positive consequences. Empirical demonstrations support clinical observations that in other instances recurring SIBs frequently are strengthened by their effectiveness in removing or reducing aversive events. These reinforcing events may be located in the external environment or may represent internal conditions. In illustration, SIBs may be strengthened because they are followed by immediate staff attention or perhaps by the immediate removal of an aversive teacher directive. In other instances the SIBs may produce a contingent reduction in physical pain or emotional distress.

Correlation Between Skill Deficits and Excessive Behavioral Responses

As noted, many persons with mental retardation have numerous deficit skill areas that may contribute in a tertiary but significant manner to excessive behavioral reactions such as SIBs. The absence or low strength of needed social and coping skills frequently influence the development and expression of excessive problem behaviors. For example, a person may become angry at a staff member but, due to deficits in verbal or other social or emotional coping skills, may express this anger by engaging in self-injury. As described later, these maladaptive reactions may become predominant modes of coping as these become highly **effective** and **efficient** functional means of removing unwanted demands or other unpleasant conditions. Another person may become self-abusive, begin to cry, and engage in aimless overactivity when confronted with various stressors due to the absence or low strength of more appropriate communicative or other social coping skills. These aberrant behaviors may become functional or serve a purpose for the person as these result in positive consequences (e.g., social feedback) or remove negative ones (e.g., peer taunts, staff directives). These thus become functional substitutes for more appropriate means of coping.

Skill Versus Performance Deficits

It is useful to distinguish between self-injurious behaviors that reflect the effects of **skill deficits,** as illustrated above, and those that reflect **performance deficits**. In the case of a skill deficit, a desired alternative coping behavior has never been learned. As a result, SIBs may occur in provoking situations as the person has no functionally equivalent alternative skills to use. In this case, the goal of a habilitation program would be that of teaching both the alternative skills and the personal motivation to use these as replacements for the SIBs.

In other instances, a desired coping skill may be in a person's repertoire, but currently is not performed. The person may not be motivated to use the skills or may be more prone to engage in SIBs as these are more effective and efficient in gaining reinforcement. Finally, **internal** (e.g., excessive anxiety, thinking about a disturbing experience) or **external** (e.g., presence of a peer, excessive noise) stimulus conditions may produce behaviors that actively compete with the performance of coping skills currently in the person's repertoire. Whenever a performance deficit is evident, the basis for the deficit would be identified and program experiences provided that specifically address these interfering factors. These program approaches are discussed in later chapters on psychosocial interventions.

Developing Individualized Interventions

Assessment data provide the basis for developing a series of hunches about current factors that contribute to self-injurious episodes. As noted, hypotheses are developed about:

- **current environmental conditions** of a psychosocial and/or physical nature (e.g., threats from peers, loud noise, new teacher);

- **personal features** of a biomedical and psychological nature (e.g., excessive anger arousal, generalized irritability associated with an organic mental syndrome, bipolar disorder, deficit coping skills); and,

- **the functions served** by the self-injurious behaviors (e.g., results in removal of task demands, produces staff distress, modulates pain or emotional distress).

In most instances of chronic SIBs, multiple hypotheses are developed about contributing factors in each of these areas, which in turn form the basis for prescribing person-specific intervention approaches. (Psychosocial and biomedical intervention procedures and the manner in which these interface with the diagnostic formulations are described in the following chapters.) In devising these diagnostic-intervention formulations, it is important to distinguish between **effective treatment** on the one hand and **symptom management and control** on the other.

Treatment, Management, and Control

A distinction is made between those biomedical and psychosocial intervention procedures designed to produce educative, training, or **treatment** effects, that is, enduring changes in biomedical, behavioral, cognitive, emotional and perceptual features that contribute to self-injury, and those designed to **manage** the occurrence or intensity/duration of the SIBs. Additionally, a distinction is made between these treatment and management procedures and other procedures used to **control** specific self-inurious episodes.

Biomedical Treatment

Biomedical intervention may produce a treatment effect by reducing or removing the internal stimulus conditions that directly influence the self-injurious behaviors. Otitis media may be treated with medication, thus eliminating the pain-produced self-injurious head and ear slapping of a person with profound mental retardation who has no functional means of communicating about or otherwise reducing his earache. A primary treatment effect may be produced by psychopharmacological intervention with neuroleptic medication during the acute phase of a schizophrenic disorder. Self-injurious symptoms occurring during this phase may reduce and disappear concomitantly with remission of the psychotic symptoms. Following reduction and even termination of the drug therapy, the behavioral symptoms may not recur due to the successful treatment, that is, reduction or elimination of the biochemical abnormality producing the schizophrenic disorder.

This biomedical treatment effect is illustrated by Ms. Balboa following a diagnosis of a bipolar mood disorder:

> *Ms. Ruthann Balboa, a person with severe mental retardation, engages in self-injurious behaviors involving face-slapping and head banging under a variety of demand conditions. However, these greatly increase in frequency and severity on an episodic basis. Careful observations of changes in biological and psychological characteristics that correlated with these episodes suggested a diagnosis of a bipolar mood disorder. Following psychopharmacological treatment of the underlying disorder, the episodic nature of Ruthann's*

> *SIBs were eliminated. She then was more responsive to psychosocial treatment of the self-injurious behaviors that occurred independently of her depression.*

Psychosocial Treatment

Psychosocial treatment refers to the use of procedures designed to **reduce** the frequency, duration, and/or intensity of SIBs and to **increase** the strength of positive functionally useful alternative skills (e.g., reacting to peer taunts in a socially appropriate manner, expressing anger through appropriate coping means). The major objective of treatment is that of producing **enduring** behavior change that will persist across time and situations. To emphasize, a psychosocial treatment program is designed to change the person's responsiveness to external and internal physical and psychological conditions that instigate and/or increase the likelihood of self-injury and to teach new socially appropriate emotional and behavioral skills that will replace the inappropriate acts.

The specific psychosocial treatment procedures selected should have both conceptual and, whenever available, empirical support for producing enduring behavior change. As an example:

> *A young man with moderate mental retardation who engages in frequent self-injurious behaviors may be provided a skills training program designed to teach him to cope with peer conflict. This treatment procedure is based on the behavior therapy concept that the SIBs are functional for the young man in terminating the peer conflict. Teaching a coping skill to serve the same function for the person as that served by the self-injury (i.e., is equally effective and efficient) should result in a reduction or elimination of these behaviors.*

As a second example:

> *Children or adults with severe developmental disabilities who engage in tantrums, self-injury, and aggression when provided tasks that are difficult for them may be taught alternative communication skills to use as functional replacements. This intervention is based on the observation that the inappropriate behaviors serve a useful communicative function. Specifically, a child may become self-injurious when directed to engage in tasks that she finds excessively difficult. As a result of the SIBs, the teacher may remove the tasks and direct her to leave the classroom to calm herself. Once she has learned a more appropriate means of communicating her dislikes for or soliciting assistance with the tasks that effectively influences the teacher to modify the task demands, the SIBs will serve no functional purpose for her and, in this situation, should reduce or disappear.*

Management of SIBs by Biomedical Intervention

Biomedical intervention also may serve a management function relative to specific SIBs. In illustration of biomedical management, psychopharmacological intervention involving drugs such as lithium or carbamazepine may reduce the setting stimulus conditions of irritability or generalized restlessness in a person with profound mental retardation and thus reduce the likelihood of SIBs under other conditions of provocation. On termination of the drug regimen, the person's irritability level and self-injurious acts may return to the preintervention level. The drug regimen thus served to reduce the SIBs by managing the setting event component of the stimulus complex involved in its instigation.

Management of SIBs by Psychosocial Interventions

Management of SIBs through use of psychosocial interventions may be **proactive** or **reactive** in nature.

Proactive procedures involve changing antecedent stimulus conditions that precede SIBs and are designed to encourage alternative prosocial actions currently available in the person's repertoire. **Reactive** procedures are initiated following the occurrence of a self-injurious episode. Even though reactive, this management procedure may prove quite valuable in minimizing the duration and severity of any specific episode. These management procedures as a group are supportive of active treatment efforts, but differ critically in function and effect as these do not in isolation produce durable reduction in the SIBs.

Proactive Psychosocial Management Procedures

In an initial **proactive** approach, psychosocial management procedures are initiated that serve to **remove** or **minimize** the effects of specific preceding conditions that instigate SIBs. As an example, a staff member who consistently provokes anger, negativism, and SIBs in a particular trainee at a work adjustment program may be reassigned to different clients. Another client who easily becomes agitated and occasionally self-injurious when directed to quickly change from one task to another may be assigned to a work activity that is routine and nonchanging. In these instances, the likelihood of becoming agitated and engaging in SIBs is reduced by managing the stimulus conditions that provoke these behaviors.

In a second **proactive** psychosocial management approach, stimulus conditions are **presented** that increase the likelihood of prosocial adaptive behaviors that replace the inappropriate action. As an example, it has been shown that providing strongly preferred reinforcers for correct responding under aversive demand conditions in a classroom results in an increase in the students' prosocial behaviors and a concomitant abrupt decrease to a low level in the previously observed high-rate aberrant behaviors. The reinforcers served to prompt prosocial behaviors that successfully competed with the self-injury and other aberrant responses.

In a third **proactive** psychosocial management procedure, self-injurious behaviors are **inhibited** by the presentation of conditions that signal the potential occurrence of negative consequences following an episode of self-injury. In illustration, providing an adolescent a reminder that occurrence of self-injury will result in loss of valued privileges may serve to inhibit the occurrence of the problem behavior.

Reactive Psychosocial Management Procedures

The final psychosocial management procedure is **reactive** in nature and used after SIBs have begun. This procedure is designed to terminate or decrease the duration and/or intensity of the current episode. Such specific approaches as redirection, removing or reducing the instigating conditions, ignoring the behavior when acknowledging it would serve to intensify it, and removing the person from the source of instigation (e.g., removing the person to a quiet area away from the provoking noisy environment) illustrate the types of reactive tactics that may serve this management function.

Management of SIBs: Summary

As indicated, the primary objective in using biomedical and psychosocial management procedures is that of reducing the occurrence of SIBs. A diagnostic assessment of self-injury in a child with severe developmental delays may reveal an increased likelihood of SIBs under conditions of specific task demands or under conditions of reduced social attention. With this diagnostic information, the occurrence of self-injurious behaviors may be reduced or even eliminated by removing these instigating conditions, that is, by never presenting task demands and/or by continually providing a rich schedule of social attention. Again, under these conditions of managing the specific stimulus conditions that instigate the self-injury, the inappropriate behavior may not occur. Whenever the controlling stimulus events of task demands and reduced social attention are reintroduced, however, the self-injury could be expected to reappear. The strength of the self-injurious behaviors in the presence of these controlling conditions has not been altered by the use of the management procedures. Durable changes could be expected only when treatment procedures are included that eliminate instigating biomedical and psychosocial conditions or actively teach and insure durable alternative prosocial responses to these controlling events.

As a second illustration, assessment may reveal that a person's episodes of agitation and self-injury could be minimized in intensity and duration if, immediately following initial signs of agitation, the person is redirected into alternative activities. The strength of these problem behaviors is not altered by this reactive management procedure; rather their disruptive features are minimized. With consistent use of this management procedure, the person may quickly become available to participate in whatever treatment experiences are provided. From a treatment perspective, this management program could be improved considerably by adding procedures that, for example, would teach the person (a) to recognize his own early signs of agitation and then (b) to self-initiate alternative activities that would reduce or remove his agitation and the subsequent self-injury.

Michael Halihan provides illustration of the contrast between a staff implemented proactive psychosocial management procedure and use of a similar procedure as treatment.

> *Functional diagnostics revealed that Mr. Halihan's disruptive outbursts of yelling, hitting himself in the head, striking out at peers, and overturning his work bench in a supported employment placement was preceded by such actions as muttering to himself, body rocking, and tapping his foot in a vigorous manner. On observing these signs, staff would suggest that Michael take a short break from his work and calm himself. This proactive psychosocial management approach resulted in a significant reduction in the number of disruptive episodes. On occasion when staff did not detect these precursors, episodes did occur. As one component of a comprehensive treatment program, Michael was taught to recognize his own signs of increased arousal and to inform staff that he needed to take a walk to calm himself. Following the teaching of self-management skills, Michael's outbursts seldom occurred.*

Behavior Control

        Behavior control refers to the use of psychosocial and biomedical procedures in a behavioral crisis to deal with out-of-control SIBs that pose a potential danger to the person and/or those in the environment. These control procedures include the use of various **physical restraints** (e.g., isolating the person in a locked space, physically holding the person, using mechanical devices such as leather belts or cuffs) and **chemical restraints** (e.g., use of a neuroleptic or benzodiazepine to sedate the person). These procedures are used in emergency situations for the sole purpose of immobilizing the individual for the duration of a current crisis, and are used only after other treatment and management procedures have failed. The purpose of behavior control procedures is neither to produce durable behavior change nor to reduce the likelihood that a current behavior episode will escalate to out-of-control status (that is, to serve as a management procedure). Rather, behavior control procedures are used to protect the person who has not responded to treatment or management procedures and already has reached an out-of-control status. His/her actions are restrained to minimize the possibility of injury to self or others.

        It is, of course, possible that some behavior control procedures (e.g., physically restraining a person's movement until control is regained) may have a treatment effect (i.e., a reinforcing or punishing effect) of increasing, or reducing, the future likelihood of the out-of-control SIBs. However, a particular control procedure used with a specific person is neither selected nor used to produce this effect.

Interrelations of Procedures

        As emphasized, intervention programs for self-injurious behaviors should have the dual objectives of teaching and/or strengthening the discriminated occurrence of personally satisfying and socially appropriate adaptive behaviors and of reducing or eliminating the self-injury. To accomplish these objectives, multimodal programs most frequently will include, in addition to treatment procedures designed to contribute to durable change, (a) those supportive biomedical and psychosocial management procedures designed to facilitate occurrence of desired behavior and to minimize occurrence of SIBs, and (b) when needed for those persons inclined to demonstrate out-of-control episodes of SIBs, behavior control components. With effective treatment procedures, however, these supportive management and control components may be minimized and faded gradually as treatment goals are accomplished and as the person is able to adapt appropriately under the normal or usual conditions of his/her usual living, work, and leisure environments.

Summary

The Multimodal Functional Model recommends an intervention plan that is diagnostically based and designed to change those current biomedical, psychological, and environmental factors assumed to contribute to the person's self-injury. As noted, a person's SIBs represent the end result of a history of experiences and a current set of conditions as these have and do interact with specific biomedical and psychological characteristics of the person. Interventions, to be successful in producing lasting effects, are derived from a set of interrelated biopsychosocial diagnostic formulations.

Specific biomedical and psychosocial conditions that contribute to the development and persistent recurrence of SIBs are discussed in Chapters 3 and 4.

THREE

Why Self-Injurious Behaviors Occur: Biomedical Influences

Introduction

A number of biomedical and psychosocial theories about factors that contribute to the origin, instigation, and maintenance of SIBs have been mentioned. While only minimal systematic attention has been devoted to factors involved in the etiology or initial onset of SIBs, theories relating to factors contributing to the habitual recurrence of these sometimes seemingly intractable problem behaviors have resulted in an extensive research and clinical literature. The various theories are not mutually exclusive and no one theory, biomedical or psychosocial, currently represents an adequate account of the initial onset and the continued occurrence of SIBs in all individuals. In fact, as noted in this chapter and the one to follow, it appears that a number of different biomedical and psychosocial factors can contribute to the initial onset and the subsequent instigation and persistence of SIBs.

In view of these potential multiple causal and maintaining determinants, the possible contributing effects of each of the factors discussed should be considered in attempts to understand and treat the SIBs of a particular individual. As illustrated, the causal and maintaining factors may be multifaceted even within the same individual. To emphasize, separate attention should be given to the presumed factors that contribute to the initial onset (etiology) of SIBs and to those influences involved in the subsequent instigation and habitual recurrence of these behaviors. This distinction is of significance in understanding SIBs as the factors associated with initial appearance may be different from those involved in their current instigation and maintenance.

Biomedical Influences

The current chapter identifies a number of biomedical factors that may contribute to an increased risk for occurrence of various aberrant behaviors, including self-injury. Alterations in physical function, both within and outside of the central nervous system (CNS), can serve as potential contributors to the initial onset, subsequent instigation, and persistent reoccurrence of SIBs. Changes as diverse as physical discomfort due to constipation and seizure-related motor behavior have all been implicated, and they highlight the need for a careful medical assessment as part of the evaluation of clients who engage in SIBs.

Physical Illness

Role of Pain and Discomfort

Localized discomfort, (e.g., headaches, cramps) as well as **generalized discomfort** (e.g., malaise, chills) may serve occasionally as the necessary stimulus condition for instigating SIBs. In many instances, maladaptive behavior may be the major means available to the person to indicate distress or physical needs.

A second potential mechanism of action relates to pain **modulation**. For example, the onset of SIBs among those individuals with severe and profound disabilities has been correlated with medical illnesses such as middle ear infections (ear slapping), headaches (head banging), blisters (biting), skin disorders (scratching). It has been suggested that the person's perception of pain can be directly attenuated by engaging in SIBs. Thus, medical treatment, which reduces the internally produced discomfort, may result in the cessation of ear slapping, head banging, biting, or scratching.

A third potential mechanism of action linking physical illness and SIBs is the generation of **aversive emotional states**. Chronic pain may produce significant emotional distress and may contribute, as a setting stimulus condition, to the likelihood that SIBs (in persons who already are prone to them) will become more frequent and intense when there is an external aggravating event such as a directive from a work supervisor or taunt from a peer. For these individuals, the combination of internal distress and external provocation represents the necessary conditions for the occurrence of SIBs. Removal or reduction of these internal influences is useful in managing the SIBs. This relationship is illustrated by Mr. Kenneth Ryan, a 25- year-old man with no speech and limited alternative communication skills:

> *Mrs. Dora Irish, a group home parent, had been encouraging Mr. Ken Ryan to complete his morning grooming. Transportation to his vocational training program would soon arrive and Mr. Ryan had not eaten breakfast or packed his lunch. As Mrs. Irish was knocking on the bathroom door, Mr. Ryan began yelling and slapping himself in the face and head. He ran into the kitchen and continued his SIBs until Mrs. Irish physically directed his hands to his side and calmed him. Although Mr. Ryan had a long-standing history of engaging in episodes of face and head slapping, the sources of aggravation initiating his SIBs typically were not apparent to Mrs. Irish and other adults in Mr. Ryan's home and program areas. Mr. Ryan refused to eat or pack his lunch but did agree to attend his vocational training program although in this setting he remained unusually irritable. After the third episode of SIBs following minor sources of aggravation, all of which occurred after his returning from trips to the rest room, staff speculated that Mr. Ryan's irritability was due to constipation. Following treatment for this presumed condition, episodes of SIBs terminated, his irritability reduced noticeably, and Mr. Ryan returned to his usual positive demeanor.*

A second example is provided by Deborah Barrett, a 26-year-old woman with an autistic disorder:

> *Ms. Barrett has a history of infrequent but intense agitated/disruptive outbursts during which she may bite peers, staff, or herself, push, pull hair, pinch, scratch, scream and refuse to participate in various aspects of her program activities which typically she finds enjoyable. Ms. Barrett also has periods of days and even weeks without any problem behaviors. Evaluation of the episodic nature of these behavioral outbursts suggests a high correlation between an increased frequency and intensity of her disruptive behaviors and her menses. Medical management of her physical distress combined with a psychosocial program involving reduction of program requirements during Ms. Barrett's periods of increased irritability resulted in a significant reduction in her agitated/ disruptive episodes. A program designed to teach alternative communication skills was initiated to provide Ms. Barrett with appropriate means of expressing her distress and related preferences.*

Role of Disturbed Physical Function

In addition, **disease states**, via metabolic disturbances (e.g., changes in blood sugar levels or electrolyte concentrations), can **alter CNS function**. These alterations in function can result in seizures, confusional states, and specific organic mental disorders (e.g., depression associated with hypothyroidism), and can influence SIBs by mechanisms to be described in the following sections.

CNS Dysfunction: Models for Understanding the Role of Neurobiological Dysfunction in Mediating SIBs

Chemical and structural disruptions of CNS function can mediate behavior in a variety of ways. The behavioral effects will depend not only upon the **site** of the disturbance and/or **impact upon the neuro-chemical function** of the brain, but also upon the **distress** produced by these disturbances and the individual's **social learning history.**

An assessment of the contribution of neurobiological dysfunction, therefore, must include a consideration of all of these factors. This model also implies that the role of disturbed brain function cannot be viewed simply in mechanistic terms, i.e., that the behavior associated with CNS factors is **always** involuntary and reflects the release of preprogrammed motor responses. **Complex behaviors carried out over time with clear functional determinants are rarely the result of involuntary motor discharges.**

| **Model 1** | Self-Injury as a Nonspecific Response to CNS Dysfunction |

Irritability (a state of excessive and easily provoked anger) can be a nonspecific sign of CNS disease and chronic forms of this mood state may be associated with brain dysfunction in persons with developmental disabilities (Reid, 1982). Irritability can serve as a setting factor, precipitating SIBs when demands are made on the affected person. Prior to the onset of a seizure, for example, the affected person may experience high levels of irritability and react to a request to complete a routine task with a self-injury. Delirium (a state of mental confusion) caused by metabolic changes, drug toxicity, and other alterations in CNS function, can contribute as setting conditions to SIBs via associated mental status changes including anxiety, restlessness, mood lability, and irritability (Wise, 1987).

| **Model 2** | Self-Injury as a Manifestation of Disrupted Psychological Operations |

Psychological operations are the basic units of mental function and include the regulation of mood states, information processing, and memory function (van Praag et al., 1990). Brain damage may result in a breakdown in these integrative processes and result in behavior abnormalities.

Rage attacks (a state of precipitous and extreme anger triggered by minor antecedents) are seen as a complication of closed head injury, for example, and represent an inability to modulate strong negative feelings and may present as acts of physical assault and SIBs. The likelihood of a rage attack occurring will be dependent on factors such as the person's level of irritability and severity of the triggering event.

Another example would be **overarousal** (a state of hypervigilance, autonomic arousal, and readiness for action) in persons with autism. It is believed to be due to sensory processing deficits associated with the disorder (Baron-Cohen, 1989; Kinsbourne, 1980). In such cases, SIBs as a form of stereotypic activity are believed to serve a dearousing effect, possibly by regulating CNS serotonergic activity via repetitive motor behavior (Jacobs, 1991).

Severe disturbances in attention and concentration can also mediate SIBs. Individuals who are highly distractible and have an impaired ability to be self-directed for more than a few minutes at a time, may perform SIBs as a way to maintain one-to-one staff contact.

| Model 3 | Self-Injury as an Involuntary Behavior |

Some cases of SIBs are believed to represent involuntary motor behavior not under the conscious control of the individuals. It has been proposed, for example, that a **supersensitivity of central D_1-dopamine receptors** with the extrapyramidal system might mediate SIBs. This supersensitivity, due to brain damage prior to or at birth, results in the childhood onset of involuntary and repetitive stereotypic movements which are self-injurious in nature (Gualtieri, 1989; Gualtieri & Schroeder, 1989). This explanation has been proposed for the compulsive self-biting associated with Lesch-Nyhan disease (see discussion to follow).

Frontal lobe seizure activity is another model for conceptualizing the role neurological dysfunction in mediating extreme forms of SIBs such as head banging, skin gouging and self-biting. Gedye (1989), for example has proposed that some SIBs represent frontal lobe seizure activity. This will be discussed in the following section.

CNS Dysfunction: Epilepsy

The role of seizures, per se, in mediating maladaptive behavior is overestimated and frequently misunderstood. Preictal confusion and irritability are more likely to mediate SIBs than the seizures themselves. Abnormal behavior during a seizure is quite rare, but may occur in partial complex seizures (temporal or frontal lobe epilepsy) (Fenwick, 1989).

Gedye (1989) has proposed that repetitive and stereotypic SIBs can be an involuntary manifestation of frontal lobe seizures. When seizures are present, there are usually associated features such as grimacing, blinking, and involuntary eye movements, e.g., eyes roll up or there is a fixed gaze:

> *A person with profound mental retardation hits his head with hands, hits jaw mostly on left, bites left hand and draws blood, bites right hand, thrusts head back quickly, kicks feet on hard surfaces. During these activities, the man stares with eyes wide open, groans, laughs for no reason (Gedye, 1989).*

CNS Dysfunction: Neurodevelopmental Disorders

The behavioral effects of neurodevelopmental disorders can be mediated through the development of space occupying lesions (e.g., tuberous sclerosis, Sturge-Webber syndrome), metabolic, brain damage (e.g., fetal malnutrition, prematurity), or genetically determined changes in CNS function (e.g., fragile X syndrome) (Szymanski et al., 1989). Their behavioral expression will be determined by both specific (e.g., structural abnormalities, associated behavioral phenotypes) and nonspecific CNS effects (e.g., disordered mood states including irritability and overarousal). Table 3.1 through 3.5 lists the diagnostic features of those neurodevelopmental disorders that typically are associated with an increased risk of SIBs.

TABLE 3.1 NEURODEVELOPMENTAL DISORDERS ASSOCIATED WITH SELF-INJURIOUS BEHAVIOR

Autistic Disorder (DSM-III-R criteria)

A. Eight symptoms/behaviors must be present including at least two from (1), one from (2), and one from (3):

1. reciprocal social interaction impairments
   a. marked lack of awareness of the interests, existence, or feelings of others
   b. lack of comfort-seeking behavior
   c. no or impaired imitation of the behavior of others
   d. no or abnormal social play
   e. gross impairment in peer friendship-making abilities

2. impaired communication skills
   a. no mode of communication
   b. abnormal nonverbal communication
   c. absence of imaginative activity movements
   d. marked abnormalities in speech production
   e. marked abnormalities in speech form/content
   f. impaired ability to initiate or sustain a conversation

3. restricted activities/manifested by any of the following
   a. stereotyped body movements
   b. persistent preoccupation with parts of objects
   c. marked distress over trivial changes
   d. need for sameness
   e. markedly restricted range of interests

B. Onset during infancy (< 36 months) or childhood (> 36 months).

TABLE 3.2 NEURODEVELOPMENTAL DISORDERS ASSOCI-
ATED WITH SELF-INJURIOUS BEHAVIOR

de Lange Syndrome

A. Developmental disabilities

B. Short stature

C. Upper and lower extremity defects (Not all findings may be present.)

D. Facial anomalies
   1. bushy eye brows and hair on upper lip
   2. small antiverted nose
   3. thin lips/small beaked nose
   4. underdeveloped jaw

TABLE 3.3 NEURODEVELOPMENTAL DISORDERS ASSOCI-
ATED WITH SELF-INJURIOUS BEHAVIOR

Fragile X Syndrome

A. Defective site on X chromosome

B. Physical anomalies (not all features will be present)
   1. large testicles
   2. protruding/large ears
   3. large hands and feet

(continued)

TABLE 3.3 NEURODEVELOPMENTAL DISORDERS ASSOCI-ATED WITH SELF-INJURIOUS BEHAVIOR (continued)

Fragile X Syndrome (continued)

    4. elongated face
    5. large head and nose
    6. arched palate
    7. high birth weight
    8. mitral valve prolapse

C. Neurological findings
    1. seizures
    2. poor motor coordination
    3. brisk reflexes

D. Psychological findings
    1. developmental disabilities
    2. emotional lability
    3. attention deficit disorder

TABLE 3.4 NEURODEVELOPMENTAL DISORDERS ASSOCI-ATED WITH SELF-INJURIOUS BEHAVIOR

Lesch-Nyhan Disease

A. Hypoxanthine-guanine phosphoribosyl transferase (HGPRT) deficiency

B. Choreoathetoid movement disorder

C. Spasticity

D. Developmental disabilities

E. Compulsive self-mutilation

TABLE 3.5 NEURODEVELOPMENTAL DISORDERS ASSOCIATED WITH SELF-INJURIOUS BEHAVIOR

Rett Syndrome

A. Normal development for first 6-18 months age followed by progressive deterioration in psychological and neurological function

B. Severe-profound developmental disabilities

C. Acquired microcephaly

D. Neurological findings (not all findings are present)
   1. loss of voluntary hand function
   2. seizures
   3. difficulty swallowing
   4. decreased muscle tone followed by progressive spasticity deformities
   5. loss of speech/communication
   6. apnea
   7. scoliosis and/or foot deformities
   8. gait disturbance

E. Stereotypic hand wringing and mouthing

Lesch-Nyhan disease, is the prototypical example of these neurodevelopmental disorders. It is a genetically determined disorder of purine metabolism in which xanthine and uric acid are built up in various body tissues (see review by Gedye, 1992). The presumed cause of SIBs is damage to the extrapyramidal system and results in not only behavioral abnormalities, but spasticity and mental retardation. As discussed in the previous section, SIBs associated with Lesch-Nyhan disease may result from dopamine$_1$-receptor supersensitivity.

In Lesch-Nyhan disease, compulsive and uncontrollable self-biting of the tongue, lips and fingers can result in severe deformities and may require constant physical restraint and, in some cases, multiple teeth extraction. Some individuals even request to be restrained, possibly to avoid the pain produced by their behavior. In addition to what appears to be involuntary SIBs, it has been suggested that some of the self-mutilation may be partially voluntary and serves to gain social attention and/or remove aversive external conditions such as staff directives.

Other neurodevelopmental disorders associated with SIBs include: autism, Cornelia de Lange syndrome, fragile X syndrome, and Rett syndrome. SIBs may reflect an attempt to modulate overarousal, e.g., fragile X syndrome (Turk, 1992), and neurological dysfunction, e.g., Rett syndrome.

CNS Dysfunction: Organic Mental Syndromes

Other causes of mental retardation such as CNS viral infection and CNS trauma (oxygen deprivation) prior to birth or during childhood are also associated with behavioral disturbances. These disturbances can best be conceptualized as organic mental syndromes, i.e., constellations of behavioral and emotional abnormalities related to brain dysfunction. As opposed to neurodevelopmental disorders, the behavior associated with organic mental syndromes usually reflect static one-time disturbances in CNS dysfunction (e.g., head trauma secondary to a forceps assisted delivery). Of course, disorders such as tuberous sclerosis and Sturge-Webber disease involve space occupying lesions and may, in turn, cause organic mental syndromes as well.

Congenital rubella infection, for example, has been associated with a behavioral syndrome characterized by irritability, overactivity, disrupted sleep, and severe SIBs and aggression (Sovner & Lowry, in press; Welch & Sovner, 1992). Another example is provided by a person in a state of chronic excitement associated with pervasive overactivity, disrupted sleep, provocative behavior, and frustration-related SIBs. These features typically begin in early childhood and are thought to reflect perinatal brain damage (Sovner & Lowry, in press).

Drug Effects

Drugs may generate or maintain SIBs by their influence on physical and mental functioning. Naturally occurring physical dysfunction is a useful model for conceptualizing the effects of drugs on behavior. Drug-induced illness, e.g., tricyclic-induced constipation, may produce nonspecific distress. Also, some psychotropic agents can lower the seizure threshold, thereby increasing the frequency of pre-ictal behavior. Other drugs may have specific neurotransmitter effects and thereby produce behavioral and psychiatric syndromes such as propranolol (Inderal) induced depression.

Side-Effects of Drugs

Drugs may directly affect mood and produce adverse emotional states, e.g., overstimulation associated with fluoxetine (Prozac) therapy (Hamilton & Opler, 1992). These, in turn, may contribute to SIBs. Of particular concern is **akathisia**, a state of motor restlessness associated with antipsychotic drug therapy (Gualtieri & Sovner, 1989). This drug side-effect is intensely uncomfortable and must be considered as a contributor to SIBs in any individual receiving an antipsychotic agent. A medical student, who had volunteered to be in a neuroendocrine study involving haloperidol (Haldol), developed akathisia and described his experience:

> With the possible exception of going on stage on an opening night, I cannot remember any feeling of anxiety so intense. Second, the sense of a foreign influence forcing me to move was dramatic (Kendler, 1976).

Another adverse reaction of particular significance is paradoxical excitement. When persons with severe and profound disabilities, especially those with perinatal trauma, are treated with sedative/hypnotics such as phenobarbital or chloral hydrate, they become

excited, i.e., restless, uncooperative, and sleepless, and engage in SIBs
(Barron & Sandman, 1985). Table 3.6 lists specific drug side-effects
and their behavioral effects.

TABLE 3.6 SOME BEHAVIORAL DRUG SIDE-EFFECTS WHICH CAN MEDIATE SELF-INJURIOUS BEHAVIORS

Adverse Reaction	Behavioral Manifestations	Implicated Drugs
akathisia	anxiety overactivity	antipsychotics
akinesia	withdrawal depression	antipsychotics
amphetamine-like irritability	jitteriness pacing	tricyclic and MAO inhibitor antidepressants, fluoxetine, and bupropion
disinhibition	increase in behavior severity	benzodiazepines
excitement	overactivity irritability	sedative/hypnotics

Drug Withdrawal Reactions

Withdrawal reactions to drug therapy represent another cause
of drug-induced behavior. The abrupt discontinuation of treatment can
result in the hyperexcitability of various neuronal systems.

Anticholinergic Withdrawal Reaction

If a drug which has anticholinergic side-effects (constipation, dry mouth, rapid heart beat) is abruptly discontinued, a withdrawal syndrome characterized by malaise, diarrhea, and decreased appetite may occur. This syndrome is uncomfortable and the distress may generate SIBs. It is typically observed with the abrupt withdrawal of tricyclic antidepressants, e.g., amitriptyline (Elavil), low potency antipsychotics, e.g., thioridazine (Mellaril), and anticholinergic antiparkinson agents, e.g., benztropine (Cogentin) (Gardos et al., 1978).

Sedative/hypnotic Withdrawal Reaction

The abrupt discontinuation of any drug which is a CNS depressant can produce a potentially life-threatening withdrawal reaction associated with mental confusion and excitement, tremulousness, and grand mal seizures. Barbiturates and other sedative/hypnotics such as chloral hydrate, and benzodiazepines including alprazolam (Xanax), clonazepam (Klonopin), and diazepam (Valium) can all produce this syndrome.

Tardive Akathisia

Tardive akathisia represents motor restlessness following the taper or discontinuation of antipsychotic drug therapy and is believed to be a form of tardive dyskinesia (Gualtieri & Sovner, 1989). Another withdrawal reaction observed to occur with the taper of low potency agents such as thioridazine (Mellaril) and chlorpromazine (Thorazine) is characterized by intense anxiety and agitation, disrupted sleep, and decreased appetite and weight loss (Gualtieri & Sovner, 1989).

Mental Illness: Overview

SIBs can be associated with mental illness by mechanisms discussed in previous sections. It is important to recognize that SIBs, with the exception of stereotypy/habit disorder, are not a primary feature of any mental illness classified in the **Diagnostic and Statistical Manual of Mental Disorders, Third Edition-Revised (DSM-III-R)** (American Psychiatric Association, 1987).

Each mental illness has specific behaviors and psychological changes, and these determine the behavioral presentation. A behavior can be associated with a mental illness in one of three main ways (Sovner, 1989).

1. **First order behavior** represents a primary manifestation of the disorder, i.e., the behavior reflects the illness itself and cannot be explained on the basis of operant or habilitative factors. Manic hyperactivity would be an example. As discussed above, self-injury is almost never a first order behavior.

2. **Second order behavior** represents the exacerbation of longstanding maladaptive behavior following the onset or recurrence of a mental illness. For example, the person who engages in self-injury which had been controlled, will begin to have high rates of the behavior with the onset of a depression (Lowry & Sovner, 1992; Sovner et al., 1993).

3. **Third order behavior** represents new behaviors which began after the onset of a psychiatric disorder and result from family or caregivers' responses to the individual. Hoarding behavior, for example, may be a feature of obsessive-compulsive disorder in persons with mental retardation. If staff intervene and prevent this behavior, it may produce significant anxiety and anger which might express itself through self-injury.

An assessment of SIBs should include a consideration of

whether a **DSM-III-R** mental illness is present. This relationship between occurrence of SIBs and the presence of a mental illness is illustrated by Mr. Sirota, a man in his thirties with profound developmental handicaps:

> *Mr. Sirota's episodes of SIBs had not been responsive to a range of behavioral and psychotropic medication interventions. He typically displayed passivity, a low energy level, restricted range of facial expressions, infrequent smiling and frequent whining. He occasionally displayed outbursts of excitement characterized by screaming, crying, and SIBs. These episodes typically occurred more frequently following incidents of frustration over delays in obtaining preferred activities. On other occasions, the precipitating events were not apparent. Based on his depressed mood and decreased activity level, a diagnosis of chronic major depression was followed by treatment with fluoxetine (Prozac). Mr. Sirota's episodes of SIBs reduced significantly as did his passivity. These changes coincided with an increase in displays of positive affect, activity level, and tolerance of frustration.*

The presence of one or more of the following findings should warrant further investigation regarding the presence of a mental illness:

- SIBs represent a new occurrence;

- Recent episodes of SIBs represent an obvious increase in frequency, duration, or intensity of chronic SIBs in the absence of any apparent psychosocial or other biomedical change that may account for the increase;

- SIBs represent only one of a number of other behavioral/ psychological symptoms which occur on a cyclical or episodic basis;

- SIBs occur in association with a disturbance of sleep, appetite or activity level;

- SIBs are associated with a pathological mood state such as depression, irritability, excitement, or overarousal.

Mood Disorders

Self-injury has been reported to be associated with major depression (Sovner & Pary, 1993; Sovner et al., 1993), and the depressed phase of bipolar disorder (Lowry & Sovner, 1992). Possible mechanisms of action include the modulation of depressed, anxious or irritable mood state and a way to terminate a state-dependent aversive condition associated with a depression-related mood state. Thus SIBs associated with depression represent a second order behavior. It is doubtful there is a suicidal intent to this behavior (Sovner & Pary, 1993). Table 3.7 presents the **DSM-III-R** criteria for major depression.

Self-injury has also been reported to occur in association with mania (Sovner & Pary, 1993). Manic irritability and overactivity may mediate the behavior which may represent a dearousal mechanism. SIBs in association with mania in a person with autism has also been reported (Steingard & Biederman, 1987). Table 3.8 presents the **DSM-III-R** criteria for Mania. Bipolar definitions are included in Table 3.9.

TABLE 3.7   DSM-III-R CRITERIA FOR MAJOR DEPRESSION

Depression of at least two weeks duration. At least five symptoms must be present and include (1) or (2):

1. depressed mood
2. decreased interest/pleasure
3. appetite/weight change

(continued)

TABLE 3.7 DSM-III-R CRITERIA FOR MAJOR DEPRESSION (continued)

4. insomnia or hypersomnia
5. psychomotor retardation/agitation
6. low energy or fatigue
7. feelings of worthlessness/inappropriate guilt
8. decreased concentration/indecisiveness
9. recurrent thoughts of death

Also, client does not meet criteria for primary psychotic illness and the mood state does not reflect a grief reaction.

TABLE 3.8 DSM-III-R CRITERIA FOR MANIA

Euphoric/elevated/irritable mood (no minimum duration necessary). At least three symptoms must be present if euphoric mood present. Four symptoms must be present if only irritable mood present.

1. inflated self-esteem/grandiosity
2. decreased need for sleep
3. more talkative/pressured speech
4. flight of ideas/racing thoughts
5. distractibility
6. increased goal directed activity/psychomotor agitation
7. excessive involvement in pleasurable activities

Client does not meet criteria for primary psychotic illness.

TABLE 3.9 BIPOLAR DISORDER DEFINITIONS

Bipolar Disorder, Type I
   The client has had at least one manic episode alone or in combination with episodes of major depression.

Bipolar Disorder, Type II
   The client has only hypomanic (a manic state of mild severity) episodes in combination with episodes of major depression.

Bipolar Disorder, Rapid Cycling Type
   The client has 4 or more episodes of either mania or depression per year. Both Type I and Type II can rapid cycle. Episode duration can range from days to months.

Bipolar Disorder, Mixed
   The simultaneous presence of manic and depressive symptoms.

Cyclothymic Disorder
   A mild form of bipolar disorder.

Anxiety Disorders

SIBs have been described as an associated feature of generalized anxiety disorder in persons with mental retardation (Ratey et al., 1989; 1991). In post-traumatic stress disorder (PTSD), SIBs are often seen in response to the hyperarousal, dissociation, numbing of emotional responsiveness, and intrusion of traumatic memories (flashbacks) which accompany the disorder (van der Kolk, 1988; van der Kolk & Saporta, 1991).

Obsessive-compulsive disorder (OCD) is characterized by intrusive ego-dystonic thoughts, anxiety, and compulsive behavior. In persons with developmental disabilities, OCD presents as repetitive and ritualistic behavior (Vitiello et al., 1989). Disruption of compulsive behavior by staff has been reported to cause aggression (Vitiello et al., 1989) and possibly SIBs. Trichotillomania (compulsive hair pulling) may reflect a dearousal mechanism or be a form of OCD. **DSM-III-R** anxiety disorders criteria are listed in Tables 3.10 through 3.13.

TABLE 3.10 DSM-III-R CRITERIA FOR GENERALIZED ANXIETY DISORDER

All three criteria must be met:

A. unrealistic or excessive anxiety or worry;
B. anxiety unrelated to a mood disorder;
C. at least 6/18 symptoms:

Motor Tension
1. trembling/shaky
2. muscle tension
3. restlessness
4. easy fatigability

Vigilance/Scanning
5. feeling keyed up/on edge
6. exaggerated startle response
7. difficulty in concentration

Autonomic Hyperactivity
8. trouble falling/staying asleep
9. irritability
10. shortness of breath/feeling smothered
11. palpitations/increased heart rate
12. sweating/cold clammy hands
13. dry mouth
14. dizziness/light-headedness
15. nausea/diarrhea, abdominal distress
16. hot flashes/chills
17. frequent urination
18. trouble swallowing/a lump in throat

TABLE 3.11 DSM-III-R CRITERIA FOR OBSESSIVE-COMPUL-SIVE DISORDER

Criteria A and B must be met.

A. Presence of either obsessions or compulsions:

Obsessions are:

   1. recurrent and persistent ideas, thoughts, or images that are intrusive and senseless
   2. the person attempts to ignore or suppress such thoughts or impulses or to neutralize them or prevent discomfort or some dreaded event
   3. the person recognizes that the obsessions are the product of his or her own mind
   4. obsessions unrelated to any other Axis I diagnosis

Compulsions are:

   1. repetitive, purposeful, and intentional behaviors that are performed in response to an obsession, or to certain rules or in a stereotyped fashion
   2. the behavior is designed to neutralize or to prevent discomfort from some event or situation
   3. the person recognizes that his or her behavior is excessive or unreasonable (may not be true for young children)

B. The obsessions or compulsions cause marked distress and are time-consuming or significantly interfere with the person's daily routine or other activities.

TABLE 3.12 DSM-III-R CRITERIA FOR PANIC DISORDER

All criteria must be met:

A. Individual has experienced panic attacks (periods of intense fear or discomfort) that were unexpected and spontaneous.

B. Individual has experienced four such attacks within a 30 day period or one or more attacks is followed by 30 day period in which there is a persistent fear of having another attack.

C. At least four of the following symptoms are present during an attack:

1. shortness of breath/smothering sensation
2. dizziness, faintness, unsteady feeling
3. palpitations or rapid heart rate
4. trembling or shaking
5. sweating
6. choking
7. nausea
8. depersonalization or derealization
9. numbness or tingling sensations
10. hot flashes or chills
11. chest pain or discomfort
12. fear of dying
13. fear of going crazy or being out of control

D. During some of the attacks, at least 4 of the symptoms in C developed suddenly and increased in intensity within 10 minutes of onset of attack.

E. There is no organic factor that is causing the disturbance.

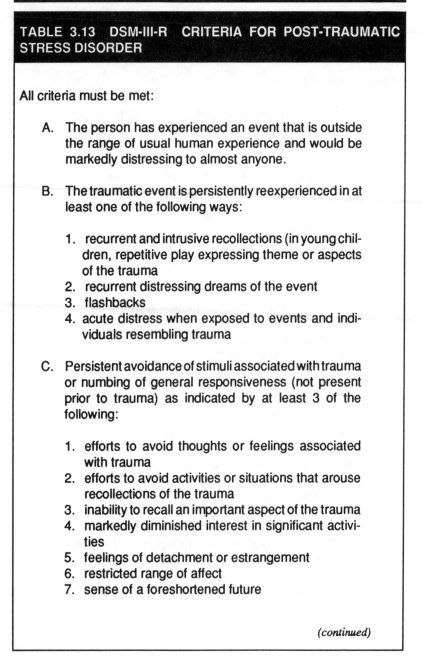

TABLE 3.13   DSM-III-R   CRITERIA   FOR   POST-TRAUMATIC STRESS DISORDER

All criteria must be met:

A. The person has experienced an event that is outside the range of usual human experience and would be markedly distressing to almost anyone.

B. The traumatic event is persistently reexperienced in at least one of the following ways:

1. recurrent and intrusive recollections (in young children, repetitive play expressing theme or aspects of the trauma
2. recurrent distressing dreams of the event
3. flashbacks
4. acute distress when exposed to events and individuals resembling trauma

C. Persistent avoidance of stimuli associated with trauma or numbing of general responsiveness (not present prior to trauma) as indicated by at least 3 of the following:

1. efforts to avoid thoughts or feelings associated with trauma
2. efforts to avoid activities or situations that arouse recollections of the trauma
3. inability to recall an important aspect of the trauma
4. markedly diminished interest in significant activities
5. feelings of detachment or estrangement
6. restricted range of affect
7. sense of a foreshortened future

(continued)

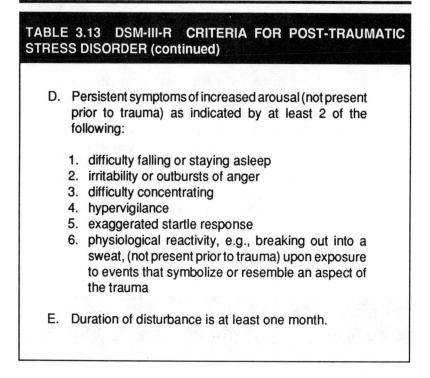

TABLE 3.13   DSM-III-R   CRITERIA   FOR   POST-TRAUMATIC
STRESS DISORDER (continued)

   D. Persistent symptoms of increased arousal (not present prior to trauma) as indicated by at least 2 of the following:

      1. difficulty falling or staying asleep
      2. irritability or outbursts of anger
      3. difficulty concentrating
      4. hypervigilance
      5. exaggerated startle response
      6. physiological reactivity, e.g., breaking out into a sweat, (not present prior to trauma) upon exposure to events that symbolize or resemble an aspect of the trauma

   E. Duration of disturbance is at least one month.

Psychoses

Self-injury in association with psychoses (including schizophrenia) is usually sporadic and usually occurs in response to delusional ideation or command hallucinations (Winchel & Stanley, 1991). The frequency of the occurrence of SIBs in conjunction with schizophrenia in developmental disabilities is unknown. It is also important to recognize that it is difficult, if not impossible, to diagnose schizophrenia in persons who are nonverbal or who function in the severe or profound range of disabilities (Reid, 1989). Without doubt, psychotic disorders are overdiagnosed in this population and the conclusion that a person's SIBs are secondary to schizophrenia or atypical psychosis is highly suspect unless there is very clearcut evidence of the presence of hallucinations or delusions.

Mr. Matson illustrates the direct effects of a mental illness on SIBs. (See Tables 3.14 and 3.15.)

With a dual diagnosis of mild mental retardation and schizophrenia, Mr. Jeffrey Matson currently resides in an acute treatment unit of a regional mental health facility. Included among a range of behavioral symptoms are infrequent but potentially dangerous episodes of self-injurious face and head slapping/punching and head banging against walls and sharp corners of furniture. These episodes appear to be instigated as a direct result of his thought and perceptual disorders. During these episodes, he can be overheard yelling repeatedly, "Stop talking to me, stop telling me to do bad things".

TABLE 3.14 DSM-III-R CRITERIA FOR SCHIZOPHRENIA

All four criteria must be met:

A.   Presence of at least 1), 2), or 3) for 1 week:

   1. any two of the following
      a. delusions
      b. prominent hallucinations
      c. incoherent thinking or loosening of associations
      d. catatonic behavior
      e. flat or grossly inappropriate affect
   2. bizarre delusions
   3. persistent auditory hallucinations

B.   marked deterioration in psychosocial functioning
C.   no evidence of a mood disorder
D.   continuous signs of disturbance for 6 months.

TABLE 3.15   PSYCHOSIS DEFINITIONS

Atypical Psychosis

An illness with unusual psychotic features that does not meet the syndromic criteria for schizophrenia, schizoaffective disorder, or other psychotic disorder. *In persons with developmental disabilities, it is often misapplied to bizarre behavior or disorganized behavior.*

Schizoaffective Disorder

An illness characterized by a manic or major depressive syndrome and also an episode of delusions and/or hallucinations without significant mood symptoms. *In persons with developmental disabilities, it is often misapplied to a bipolar or major depressive illness.*

Tourette Disorder

Tourette disorder is a neuropsychiatric illness characterized by involuntary motor and vocal tics that are variable in anatomical location and intensity, and has been reported to occur in association with developmental disabilities (Gedye, 1991; Reid, 1984) and autism (Burd et al., 1987). Table 3.16 presents the **DSM-III-R** criteria for Tourette disorder. Tourette disorder is also associated with SIBs (Gedye, 1991; Robertson et al., 1989). Robertson et al., (1989) suggested that up to one-third of persons with Tourette disorder manifest some form of SIBs. It is unclear, however, how much of this behavior reflects involuntary motor behaviors vs. obsessional thinking and/or nonspecific irritability/hostility which have also been reported with this disorder (Robertson et al., 1989).

Recent work suggests that persons with Tourette disorder have premonitory urges of an impending tic and they may initiate motor behavior to relieve the urge (Lechman et al., 1993). Such a mechanism of action may be at work in SIBs associated with Tourette disorder in persons with developmental disabilities.

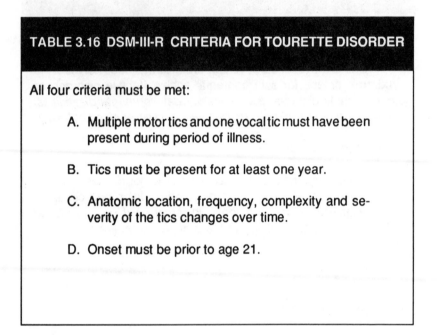

TABLE 3.16 DSM-III-R CRITERIA FOR TOURETTE DISORDER

All four criteria must be met:

    A. Multiple motor tics and one vocal tic must have been present during period of illness.

    B. Tics must be present for at least one year.

    C. Anatomic location, frequency, complexity and severity of the tics changes over time.

    D. Onset must be prior to age 21.

Attention-Deficit Hyperactivity Disorder

In persons with developmental disabilities, SIBs may occur with attention-deficit hyperactivity disorder (ADHD). (See Table 3.17.) The SIBs are associated with such features as irritability, low frustration tolerance, and emotional volatility. In addition, the need to maintain direct staff supervision may also result in SIBs (Hurley & Sovner, 1991).

TABLE 3.17 DSM-III-R CRITERIA FOR ATTENTION-DEFICIT HYPERACTIVITY DISORDER

All of the following criteria must be met:

A. A disturbance six months or longer in duration with at least eight of the following:

1. fidgets
2. has difficulty remaining seated when required to do so
3. easily distracted
4. has difficulty awaiting turn in games or groups
5. often blurts out answers before question completed
6. has difficulty following through on instructions from others
7. has difficulty sustaining attention
8. often shifts from one uncompleted activity to another
9. has difficulty playing quietly
10. often talks excessively
11. often interrupts or intrudes on others
12. often does not seem to listen to what is being said
13. often loses things necessary to or for tasks and activities
14. often engages in physically dangerous activities

B. Onset before 7-years-old

C. Does not meet criteria for pervasive developmental disorder.*

*ADHD in association with autism has been reported (Kerbeshian & Burd, 1991).

Organic Mental Syndromes

Central nervous system (CNS) dysfunction can result in significant alterations in behavior. They typically occur in individuals with mental retardation caused by CNS viral infection (e.g., congenital rubella) and space occupying lesions (e.g., tuberous sclerosis). Disorders either manifest as classic psychiatric disorder, (e.g., depression) or as exaggerations of normal stress responses (e.g., rage attacks, irritability). Problems suggestive of an organic mental syndrome include: 1) pervasive overactivity; 2) chaotic sleep pattern; 3) distractibility; 4) irritability; 5) mood lability; 6) overarousal; and 7) rage attacks. Table 3.18 presents the DSM-III-R criteria for organic brain syndromes.

TABLE 3.18 DSM-III-R CRITERIA FOR ORGANIC MENTAL SYNDROMES

Behavior is attributed to brain dysfunction

    A. Evidence of a specific brain dysfunction

    B. Absence of another **DSM-III-R** Axis I diagnosis or a pervasive developmental disorder

---

Personality Disorders

Disturbances in personality, particularly borderline personality disorder (BPD), can be associated with SIBs. Such self-injurious acts as cigarette burns, sandpapering the face, cuts on the body, arm- and head-banging, scratching oneself with fingernails, and dripping acid on the hands have been described as occurring among self-destructive persons with BPD (Gardner & Cowdry, 1985).

Summary

A range of biomedical factors may be viewed as risk or predisposing factors that increase the likelihood of the initiation and recurrence of SIBs when other primary instigating conditions are present. In some instances, self-injury may represent a direct or primary manifestation of a biomedical condition and occurs independently of other biomedical or psychosocial instigating influences. Prescriptive intervention is based on a comprehensive assessment of the type and degree of influence of relevant biomedical factors.

FOUR

Why Self-Injurious Behaviors Occur: Psychosocial Influences

Introduction

While psychodynamic theories have provided some cursory attention to self-injury, these theories appear to have minimal applicability to understanding the basis for or providing specific direction to treatment of these problem behaviors in those with mental retardation. The major contributions have come from operant learning theory that contends that self-injury represents a learned behavior maintained by its consequences.

Learned Behavior: Positive Reinforcement

After initial onset, SIBs may gain increased functionality and thus occur with consistency under specific instigating stimulus conditions because these behaviors result in valued social, activity, and/or tangible consequences. This view represents the **reinforcement-motivated hypothesis** of self-injury.

Types of Reinforcing Conditions

SIBs may be learned because they serve to signal the occurrence of such reinforcing social events as attention, concern, or physical contact. It is not unusual, especially following severe self-abuse, for staff or family to comfort the person or to attempt to prompt distraction by providing special attention, food, or a favored object or activity. As a result, SIBs may become functional in insuring that desired attention, physical contact, or other forms of social interaction will occur. In other instances, the SIBs may be maintained as they result in such reinforcing consequences as access to preferred activities and items such as food, toys, or other tangibles. This hypothesis would suggest intervention approaches directed at teaching functionally equivalent prosocial behaviors as means of gaining these reinforcing events. Illustrations of these program approaches are provided in Chapter 8.

Communication Hypothesis

In individuals with severe mental retardation, limited communication skills, and few alternative social behaviors, SIBs may be one of the few consistent means of insuring social feedback or of communicating one's needs. Some writers in fact suggest that severe behavior problems, including SIBs, may serve the same functions as socially acceptable forms of verbal and nonverbal communication. The SIBs may represent functionally equivalent forms of communicating wishes and concerns. This **communication hypothesis** of SIBs formed the basis for understanding Mr. Mark Kaplan's behavior problems:

Mr. Kaplan, a 27-year-old adult with profound mental retardation, limited social skills, and without speech, engaged in episodic bouts of agitated face slapping, head banging, and screaming. Following close observation of the conditions under which these behaviors occurred, it was noted that these most frequently occurred following periods of isolation from social contact. It was speculated that Mr. Kaplan's SIBs occurred as these insured immediate staff attention and thus met his need for social stimulation. A program of insuring that no period in excess of 20 minutes lapsed throughout the day without personalized social stimulation resulted in a significant reduction in Mr. Kaplan's SIBs. Following demonstration of the function served by the SIBs, a program was initiated of teaching Mr. Kaplan alternative communication skills of obtaining social attention.

This explanation for SIBs as a nonverbal mode of communication emphasizes the need, as noted, to replace the SIBs with **alternative functionally equivalent forms of social or communicative skills** of obtaining individually relevant positive consequences and, as discussed in the following section, of reducing, terminating, or avoiding conditions that are aversive to the person. For the individual with minimal functional social or verbal skills, this would involve teaching the person specific other means of expressing his or her needs or wishes through appropriately initiating social contact or through the use of verbal or nonverbal communication skills. To emphasize, this communication hypothesis of SIBs results in an educative skill development focus of intervention. These new communicative skills serve to produce the same or similar results for the person. Illustrations of programs designed to teach functional equivalent skills of communication are provided in Chapter 8.

Learned Behavior: Negative Reinforcement

As suggested, SIBs also may represent learned behaviors that are strengthened and maintained by negative reinforcement through the reduction or termination of unpleasant situations or events. This **escape/avoidance hypothesis** suggests that SIBs become functional as a means of escaping from currently present aversive conditions or avoiding anticipated unpleasant situations. The person with limited alternative means of expressing or communicating his or her displeasure may discover that, whenever SIBs occur, the deprivation or demand is reduced , postponed, or removed. This functional relationship is illustrated by Miss Heather.

Miss Katherine Heather, a 15-year-old adolescent with profound mental retardation and minimal communication and social skills, wore a helmet unless closely supervised to protect her from self-injury during frequent agitated/disruptive episodes. Close observation of Miss Heather's severe episodes of face slapping, scratching, and associated loud

> *screaming suggested that these were being main-*
> *tained as these removed her from various situations.*
> *As one example, following 10-15 minutes in program*
> *activities that required her to remain seated and*
> *engage in prevocational tasks, Miss Heather fre-*
> *quently would engage in agitated/disruptive behav-*
> *iors that resulted in her removal from the room. A*
> *program designed to teach Miss Heather alternative*
> *means of communicating her dislikes, combined with*
> *program approaches providing her with options of*
> *selecting her prevocational activities from among a*
> *variety of available ones, resulted in a significant*
> *reduction in her agitated/disruptive and self-injurious*
> *episodes.*

Types of Aversive Conditions

The stimulus conditions that may function as negative reinforcers (those motivating events for SIBs) vary considerably and can be
quite idiosyncratic. These aversive conditions may include periods of
minimal reinforcement, overstimulation, attempts by others to initiate
social contact, physical pain, psychological distress, medical examina-
tions, termination of social contact, staff or task demands, training tasks
that have minimal value to the person, or reduced social contact. It is
not uncommon for the same stimulus condition to function as a positive
reinforcer for one person but as a negative reinforcer for another. As one
example, social attention or physical touch may be positive for some and
quite aversive to others.

It often is observed that individually specific aversive conditions
such as unwanted demands, contact, or deprivations typically produce
strong emotional responses which in turn may increase the aversiveness
of these. Again, the person may escape from or reduce these aversive
social events, pain, distress, deprivation states, or demands for low
preference activities and associated negative emotional arousal, even
though typically only temporarily, following an episode of self-injury.

SIBs as Avoidance Behavior

In other instances, SIB's may occur when the person is exposed to stimuli that are discriminative for future aversive stimulation, and thus serve to avoid these completely. The appearance of a teacher to escort a child to a classroom in which she previously has provided aversive task-demands and physical prompts illustrates this avoidance operation. Following SIBs, the teacher concludes that the child is too upset to benefit from the school experience and returns to the classroom without the child. As a result, the SIBs are strengthened through negative reinforcement, that is, through the removal of the aversive directive to attend class. In this manner, the person learns that SIBs, although potentially painful, result in avoidance of other future unpleasant experiences.

In summary, this escape/avoidance explanation for SIBs suggests a specific program emphasis:

- on decreasing the aversive features of those persons, situations, or activities that result in SIBs;

- of teaching the person alternative and functionally equivalent means of communication or expressing his or her needs or wishes; and/or,

- of teaching other specific skills of coping with the aversive conditions.

Illustrations of each of these program approaches are provided in Chapter 8.

Learned Behavior: Sensory Stimulation

It has been demonstrated that in some instances self-injurious behavior may be maintained by the resulting **sensory stimulation**. Such behaviors as poking and pressing on the eye produce visual stimulation; head banging and face slapping produce auditory, proprioceptive and tactile stimulation, as do such behaviors as scratching or pinching. Some persons with severe and profound levels of mental retardation, with limited social behaviors, and/or with sensory and neurological difficulties thus may resort to SIBs to provide valued sensory stimulation. Some writers refer to the resulting stimulation as providing **sensory reinforcement**. Others prefer the term **automatic reinforcement** to reflect the notion that SIBs may be maintained as a result of the natural consequence of responding. This latter concept leaves open the possibility that the maintaining contingency may reflect either positive or negative reinforcement. Automatic negative reinforcement typically would involve reduction in aversive stimulus conditions arising from biomedical conditions. As examples, the distress associated with an ear infection or a dysphoric mood state may be temporarily attenuated by ear or head hitting or other forms of SIBs.

Some theorists suggest that violent contact as in face slapping or head banging increases the sensory sensitivity of the tissue involved. Repeated SIBs thus insure immediate heightened sensory input and reinforcement. Finally, it also has been suggested that repeated self-injurious behaviors may produce nerve damage which, in turn, necessitates more intense hitting, scratching, or pinching in order to experience the sensory feedback. These suggestions are offered to account for the observation that over time, self-injurious acts frequently become more intense.

This sensory stimulation hypothesis suggest that:

- attention be given to the sensory modalities involved in the SIBs;

- alternative sources of similar stimulation be provided on a frequent and routine basis; and,

- alternative behaviors be taught as a means of obtaining preferred sensory stimulation or of reducing aversive biomedical conditions.

Illustrations of these program approaches are included in the discussion of reinforcement-motivated and escape-motivated SIBs in Chapter 8.

Self-Restraint

A frequently occurring behavior among those with chronic SIBs is that of self-restraint. Self-restraint refers to self-initiated behaviors that restrict or prevent motion of one or more of their body parts, e.g., wrapping body parts in clothing, objects, or other body parts. In other instances, individuals may request or self-position themselves in physical or mechanical restraints. It appears that these persons enjoy physical restraints such as arm splints or hand or arm restraints. When these are removed, the person becomes noticeably upset and seems to welcome reapplication of restraints following periods of freedom from them. Some writers report that 95% of self-restraining individuals also engage in self-injury.

Speculations about the etiology of and the variables maintaining self-restraint offer hypotheses involving negative reinforcement, stimulus control, and self-restraint as a conditioned reinforcer.

| Negative Reinforcement Hypothesis |

There is some data support for the negative reinforcement hypothesis that self-restraint is reinforced through the termination, delay, or avoidance of self-injurious behaviors. Self-restraint reduces the aversive experiences of self-injurious episodes by delaying or terminating the SIBs. Other writers, using the negative reinforcement hypothesis to explain why some persons actively seek physical or mechanical restraints, suggest that SIBs following staff-imposed demands that have resulted in restraints may in turn effectively remove the unpleasant demands. The SIBs thus may function as an escape from demands of staff into the restraint condition.

Stimulus Control Hypothesis

While not inconsistent with the negative reinforcement hypothesis, the stimulus control hypothesis suggests that self-restraint serves as a discriminative stimulus for injury-free behavior. This hypothesis accounts for the observation that in some instances of self-restraint the behaviors are not physically incompatible with the person's specific self-injurious activities. These have been referred to as "symbolic restraints."

Conditioned Reinforcer Hypothesis

Finally, some writers suggest that self-restraints acquire conditioned reinforcer properties through repeated pairing with escape from the aversive experiences of SIBs.

The literature on self-restraint raises the possibility that these behaviors, however bizarre they may appear, may serve the functions of terminating, delaying, or avoiding SIBs. If the self-restraints are prevented from occurring without initially providing the person some alternative means of controlling the SIBs, the self-injurious acts may actually increase. A recent review of theories and treatment of self-restraint by Schroeder and Luiselli (1992) is recommended for the interested reader.

Summary

Psychosocial theories and supporting data may be divided into those that relate to the etiology or initial onset of SIBs and those that describe the manner in which these behaviors become habitual in occurrence in the presence of specific stimulus conditions. Concepts of overarousal and homeostasis have been offered as contributors to the initial onset of SIBs. Once initiated the SIBs may become habitual as these consistently produce such positive consequences as social attention or physical contact. For some, the sensory feedback resulting from SIBs may serve as the reinforcing consequence that maintains these behaviors. As a result of this learning history, SIBs come under the instigating influence of those stimulus conditions that signal the potential availability of desired consequences. In other instances, the SIBs may become functional in removing or minimizing various aversive conditions such as directives from others, physical contact, physical pain, psychological distress, a boring task or activity, conditions of overstimulation, or the presence of specific persons. The frequently observed associated behavior of self-restraint may become functional in terminating, delaying, or avoiding staff demands and/or the aversiveness associated with SIBs.

A recurring theme in the psychosocial literature is the absence or limitations in functional or alternative language skills of communicating emotional states, needs and wishes. As a result, a program emphasis of actively teaching alternative functionally equivalent communication skills is indicated.

In Chapter 5, a number of biomedical and psychosocial intervention guidelines are offered to address, in a general manner, a range of potential primary, secondary, and tertiary conditions that may contribute to self-injury.

FIVE

Intervention Guidelines for Self-Injurious Behaviors

General Treatment and Management Guides: Biomedical

Recall that SIBs, while only infrequently instigated directly by biological factors, may nonetheless reflect the influences of a range of biomedical and psychiatric disorders. Medical and psychiatric interventions for specific abnormalities and disorders can contribute to the reduction in SIBs by removing or minimizing the internal primary and secondary instigating conditions and by reducing tertiary influences. As an initial approach in instances of acute presentation of SIBs as well as in instances of a significant increase in chronic SIBs that appear unrelated to environmental or other psychosocial changes, a medical evaluation should be undertaken. As SIBs, especially in those persons with severe and profound mental retardation and minimal effective communication skills, may reflect the effect of physical pain or discomfort, identification and treatment of the underlying physical conditions producing these states may be effective in management of the SIBs.

General Treatment and Management Guides: Psychosocial

A number of psychosocial treatment and proactive behavior management approaches offer promise of reducing the frequency and severity of SIBs. These include improving the general quality of environmental experiences provided, removing or minimizing general and specific conditions of instigation, and presenting the person with a general active treatment program experience designed to teach and support a range of communication, self-care, social, work, and leisure skills.

Improving General Environmental Quality

Many persons presenting severe and chronic SIBs have an extremely limited repertoire of functional skills. If left without routine structure, the person is likely to excessively use the few functional behaviors (e.g., SIBs) that effectively produce changes in the environment. Improvement in the quality and range of physical and psychosocial environmental conditions through providing on a consistent basis (a) valued social feedback on a frequent and noncontingent basis and (b) a range of objects (e.g., toys to manipulate that provide sensory feedback) and events that stimulate active sensory and motoric involvement holds promise of reducing the motivational basis for the self-injury. Studies have demonstrated that, for those who do engage in SIBs, lower levels of these behaviors typically are observed in those environments in which objects for exploration or manipulation are present, activities resulting in sensory stimulation such as swimming or listening to music are available, aversive directives or demands are minimal, and reinforcement for behaviors incompatible with self-injury is frequent. Other studies have shown that SIBs in children with severe and profound mental retardation occur less frequently following positive interpersonal interactions and more frequently following periods of no interpersonal interactions.

This environmental enrichment approach also may strengthen a range of specific adaptive skills. In general, an enriched environment that provides a range of social, sensory, and activity stimulation will serve to initiate and reinforce alternatives to acts of self-injury. Miss Reva Glaser illustrates these observations:

Miss Glaser, an adolescent with profound cognitive and communication skill deficits, engaged in frequent episodes of SIBs consisting of head banging, hitting herself in the face and head area, and hand biting.

These episodes had increased following arrival of two additional peers in her group home that resulted in less frequent individual attention from her group home parents. The SIBs were reduced significantly following initiation of a procedure of routinely (minimum of six times per hour) providing personalized attention. Additionally, staff became more attentive to Miss Glaser's pre-self-injury signs of arousal and would relate to her more routinely when these attempts at communicating her wishes were detected. Finally, with consultation assistance from a language therapist, a program was initiated to teach Miss Glaser a functionally equivalent means of requesting attention and expressing her needs and wishes to others.

Minimizing Conditions of Instigation of SIBs

A number of different conditions may influence the occurrence of SIBs. As a general management strategy, conditions of frustration should be minimized. Such conditions as dietary control, loud noise, staff or program demands, invasion of personal space, excessive activity level of others in the immediate environment, pain, hunger, thirst, fearfulness, change of routine, and anxiety over being around strangers or being taken to unfamiliar places are some of the common conditions that create negative emotional arousal. These conditions may either serve as discriminative or setting events for SIBs. Removing or minimizing these and other commonly occurring sources of agitated arousal may serve to manage the occurrence of SIBs.

As examples of how this may be accomplished, staff may:

- minimize changes in routine;

- insure that usual (expected) positive consequences such as meals, activities, and programs are available without undue delay;

- supervise groups of individuals to insure that excessive frustration is not produced by peers invading the personal space or interfering with the possessions of others; and,

- insure that personal possessions are safeguarded and readily accessible for use.

As the specific events that influence the initiation and maintenance of SIBs are unique to each person, careful observation is needed for effective individualized program intervention. In illustration:

> *In recent observations in a work training program of a nonverbal young woman with profound mental retardation, it became evident that her vigorous and repetitive face-slapping behavior occurred mostly whenever her instructor would terminate interaction with her and begin talking to other trainees. This correlation between SIBs and termination of social attention was surprising to the instructor as he was unaware that the young woman valued his attention. Changes in his interaction patterns resulted in a reduction in the SIBs.*

Providing an Active Treatment Program

Providing an active treatment program designed to teach a range of communication, self-care, social, work when appropriate, and leisure skills greatly increases the routine attainment of valued social, activity, tangible, and sensory feedback. These skills also will be available to remove or minimize aversive conditions that may set the occasion for SIBs.

Mr. Bradford Hamilton illustrates the effects on SIBs when provided an environment that permitted him to become an active participant and to experience some valued control over aspects of his world.

Mr. Hamilton, severely physically and cognitively impaired and confined to a wheelchair, is greatly restricted in functional skills of influencing his physical and social environment. When placed in a work training program that required him to engage in activities that were difficult for him to master, he became highly agitated and engaged in episodes of severe head butting and biting his lips. Development of adaptive equipment that permitted him to control aspects of the work tasks through use of head/neck movements resulted in an immediate elimination of the SIBs. Mr. Hamilton now had a means of effectively participating in the work environment and soon began to express consistent positive affect relative to his work skills and the money that he now could earn in this setting. Reductions in SIB episodes in other settings was also accomplished by using similar prosthetic devices to control other aspects of his environment such as turning his radio-cassette and his television on and off.

Reactive Behavior Management Approaches: Psychosocial

In addition to these treatment and proactive management procedures, the following reactive management procedures may be valuable in **terminating** specific self-injurious episodes and in prompting the person to engage in alternative activities. The reactive approaches to management of SIBs should be used as adjuncts to more intensive general and specific proactive management and treatment program approaches.

Ignore Completed Episodes

If the self-injurious episode has been completed (e.g., the

person has stopped his head banging), it is best to completely ignore that specific episode. If attention in the form of reprimand or sympathy follows the SIBs, this consequence may be reinforcing. If the self-injurious episode has produced an injury that requires medical care, this should be provided with minimal empathic personal attention. Following medical care, direct the person into an appropriate activity, remove any current source of provocation if evident, and then provide the person with warm personal attention following his or her involvement in alternative activities. Additionally, insure that attention similar in duration and quality is provided on a consistent basis at other times temporally distant from the SIBs.

Ignore Minor Episodes

If SIBs are occurring but are of minor frequency, duration, and/or intensity and are unlikely to produce physical injury, ignore these. After the episode has terminated, redirect the person into alternative activities and provide positive feedback. Develop hypotheses about the instigating conditions and modify these in order to minimize future occurrence. If the SIBs are prolonged in duration or severe in intensity, however, ignoring the behaviors is not appropriate as these are likely to continue until intervention is provided.

Minimize Attention When Intervention Is Necessary

If intervention is necessary to protect the person from possible injury and/or to terminate lengthy self-injurious episodes, the physical intervention should be as minimal as needed to manage the episodes. Do not provide any unnecessary social attention, e.g., do not talk to or look at the individual any more than needed. For some individuals, a factor contributing to the maintenance of SIBs is the resulting personal attention that these produce.

If it becomes necessary, for example, to use such physical restraints as a helmet, mitts, or arm splints due to the intensity and severity of the SIBs, apply these with minimal social attention or physical feedback. Do not talk to the person, do not touch the person any more than needed to apply the restraint, and keep interaction at a minimum. When restraints are being removed, follow the same approach of minimal social and physical feedback.

Redirect Into Alternative Activities

To emphasize, these reactive management approaches are designed to terminate the self-injurious episode and to redirect the person into proactive management and treatment experiences. Insure that whenever these reactive procedures are used, the person is approached on numerous other occasions when SIBs are not occurring. On these other occasions provide the person with the type and quality of social interaction of most value to him or her. These experiences may serve to offset the potential reinforcement associated with the management procedures and at the same time, will provide the person with valued social attention and physical/sensory stimulation.

Summary

General biomedical and psychosocial treatment and management approaches to self-injury include medical screening and improvement in the type, range, and quality of psychosocial experiences provided those with chronic problems. When unsucccessful, these general approaches are followed by initiation of a comprehensive diagnostic assessment as a basis for formulating an individualized integrated biopsychosocial intervention program.

Methods of obtaining assessment information, the process of developing a set of diagnostic-intervention formulations and, finally, guides for translating these into a Multimodal Integrated Intervention Plan are described in Chapter 6.

SIX

Multimodal Functional Diagnostics

Introduction

Self-injury of a chronic nature is one of the more difficult problem behaviors to eliminate completely. For individuals who do not respond to the general treatment and management approaches described in the previous chapter, a comprehensive and individualized multimodal functional diagnostic assessment is needed.

In this functional diagnostic endeavor, it is important to remember that the SIBs of a specific individual may reflect a variety of influences of a biomedical and psychosocial nature. Unless diagnostically-based interventions remove or reduce individually relevant provoking and maintaining conditions, or unless the person is taught alternative effective and efficient ways of coping with these, the SIBs are likely to continue. This suggests that knowledge of the physical and psychosocial stimulus conditions (both external and internal) under which SIBs have an increased likelihood of occurrence offers direction to program procedures designed to reduce or eliminate these and thus to prevent or manage the SIBs. Information about various psychological features of the person, such as the presence or absence of alternative communication and coping skills and the type and range of activities or events preferred by the person, is useful in devising teaching programs for strengthening alternative functionally equivalent behaviors. Identification of the maintaining positive or negative reinforcers of the behavior offers direction in selection of condition-specific procedures for decreasing the strength of the self-injury.

In sum, the multimodal functional diagnostic assessment is designed to (a) identify the types and relative influences of those primary and secondary external and internal situations and conditions that, when present, increase the likelihood of SIBs, (b) provide a data base for hypotheses about the specific consequences that serve to strengthen and maintain these behaviors, and (c) identify tertiary environmental and personal characteristics that contribute indirectly to the occurrence and continuation of self-injury.

Developing a Multimodal Integrated Intervention Plan

As described in earlier chapters, assessment activities that identify correlations or covariations between SIBs and specific biomedical and psychosocial events or conditions represent an essential base for guiding the development of an effective Multimodal Integrated Intervention Plan (MIPP) (Figure 6.1). In this process, specific interventions are derived directly from specific diagnostic formulations about the instigating and maintaining biomedical, psychological, and socioenvironmental influences.

This process of developing a MIIP involves the following steps:

Step 1. Descriptive analysis is completed of the primary, secondary, and tertiary instigating and related maintaining influences. A diagnostic worksheet depicting these conditions is presented in Figure 6.2. This worksheet provides a common focus for diagnostic staff representing different professional and/or content areas. This descriptive analysis results in a set of diagnostic formulations about the specific and relative effects of each condition identified. As illustrations, a physician's evaluation of a 23-year-old client with profound mental retardation, who is reported to have irregular occurrence of her menses, may indicate considerable physical distress associated with menses. This physical distress is hypothesized to serve as a secondary instigating condition for the client's SIBs. This observation supports the report of the house parent that the woman's SIBs are cyclic in nature and appear to worsen during her menses. The psychologist reports that the SIBs occur under the antecedent conditions of corrective feedback, task demands, and changes in scheduled routines, and hypothesizes that

Multimodal Integrated Intervention Plan

Client: _____
Record No.: _____
Date: _____
Staff: _____

Target Symptoms

1. _Self-injurious behaviors_
2. _____
3. _____
4. _____
5. _____

	Diagnostic Hypotheses	Diagnostically-based Interventions	Staging Plan	Expected Change (Type/magnitude/ time)	Data (Type/Schedule)	Responsible Staff; Review Schedule
Medical Formulations*						
Psychiatric Formulations						
Psychological Formulations						
Socioenvironmental Formulations						

*Refers to medical conditions (other than those of a psychiatric or neuropsychiatric nature) that are presumed to contribute to the target symptoms.

Figure 6.1 Multimodal Integrated Intervention Plan Format

Multimodal Functional Disagnostics Worksheet

(Check one)

Medical	Psychiatric	Psychological/ Habilitative	Socioenvironmental

Client:
Record No:
Date:
Staff:

Target Symptoms
1. *Self-injurious behaviors*
2.
3.
4.

		Instigating Influences			Consequences/Functions				Interventions	
		Primary (Discrimina-tive) Events	Secondary (Setting) Events	Tertiary (Deficits/ Pathologies)	Positive Events Presented	Aversive Events Removed	Sensory Feedback	Other	Treatment	Manage-ment; Control
Environ-mental	Physical									
	Psychosocial									
Personal	Biomedical									
	Affective									
	Cognitive									
	Perceptual									
	Motoric									
	Social/Coping									
	Communication									
	Motivational									
	Personality									

Figure 6.2. Multimodal Functional Diagnostional Diagnostics Worksheet

the SIBs result in intermittent escape from these conditions. Further, it is reported that the influence of these antecedents on producing the SIBs waxes and wanes. The teacher reports the absence of effective functional communication skills and suggests this as a potential tertiary influence.

In summary, these separate initial observations offered by different staff using the diagnostic worksheet as a guide suggest an increase in frequency and severity of SIBs under the primary instigating conditions (corrective feedback, task demands, and changes in scheduled routines) when the secondary setting condition of physical distress associated with menses is present. Further, the SIBs serve a communicative function for the client in the absence of skills to more appropriately express her concerns.

The last section of the worksheet includes spaces for recording initial impressions about interventions related to the diagnostic hunches and further to separate these into treatment, management, and control categories. The process of interfacing various categories of interventions with related diagnostic hunches thus is begun early in assessment.

Step 2. A Specific Discipline Diagnostic-Intervention Formulations Worksheet (Figure 6.3) is used by each staff involved in the assessment to summarize the information obtained in Step 1. To illustrate the translation of diagnostic hypotheses (Column A) into diagnostically-based interventions (Column B), the physician may suggest a means of managing the SIBs through use of various medications to increase the regularity of menses and to ease the physical distress present preceding and/or during menses. These interventions address the hypothesized secondary (setting) instigating influences of physical distress. The psychologist may suggest that task demands and changes in scheduled routines be reduced or minimized immediately prior to and during menses, thus offering a means of managing the SIBs through reducing or eliminating the hypothesized primary instigating events. Under the assumption that the SIBs serve a communicative function, the teacher may suggest that functional communication training be initiated in order to provide the client with an alternative means of expressing her concerns when in a state of physical distress. As these skills develop and become effective in removing or reducing the

Specific Discipline Diagnostic-Intervention Formulations Worksheet

(Check one)

Medical	Psychiatric
Psychological/ Habilitative	Socioenvironmental

Client: _____
Record No: _____
Date: _____
Staff: _____

Target Symptoms

1. _Self-injurious behaviors_
2. _____
3. _____
4. _____
5. _____

Diagnostic Hypotheses (A)	Diagnostically-based Interventions (B)	Staging Plan (C)	Expected Change (Type/magnitude/time) (D)	Date (Type/Schedule) (E)	Responsible Staff: Review Schedule (F)

Figure 6.3. Specific Discipline Diagnostic-Intervention Formulations Worksheet

instigating conditions, it is reasoned that the SIBs will in turn become nonfunctional.

The reader is encouraged to consult the following chaper on Biomedical Treatment Paradigms and an article by Sovner and Hurley (1992) for discussion of guidelines for developing diagnostic-intervention formulations involving psychotropic drug therapy.

Following development of these diagnostic-intervention formulations, suggestions are made by each person completing the multimodal assessment about the timing or staging of the various interventions. In order to evaluate the effects of specific interventions, it may be necessary to initiate only one intervention at any given time (Column C). After determining the effects of this intervention, it may be deleted or other interventions added to address other instigating or maintaining influences.

Predictions are included in Column D relative to the results expected from each intervention along with a time frame within which these changes would be expected to occur. In Column E, the types of assessment procedures required to evaluate the effects of interventions are noted. These frequently represent extensions of those used during the initial assessment process. In other instances, additional procedures may be required to assess more precisely the predicted effects of specific interventions. For example, a diagnostic hypothesis of an anxiety disorder serving as a setting condition for SIBs may result in a related recommended intervention involving psychotropic medication. An assessment procedure directly addressing changes in the anxiety disorder will be needed to evaluate the effects of the intervention. The drug therapy may produce reduction in anxiety symptoms but have no effect on the frequency or severity of the SIBs. In this scenario, the medication could be tapered off as an ineffective medication for the SIBs.

Finally, in Column F, staff responsible for program implementation and data collection are included along with a suggested schedule for routine review of the effects of interventions.

Step 3. The diagnostic-intervention formulations and related information completed by various members involved in the assessment and program development process are meshed into a single MIIP as depicted earlier in Figure 6.1. This final and critical step is described following discussion of various assessment procedures useful in conducting the descriptive analysis.

Clinical (Descriptive) Analysis

Methods of gathering descriptive information include the use of (a) unstructured interviews and informal direct observation, (b) checklists, rating scales, and questionnaires, (c) structured interviews, and (d) structured direct observation in the person's natural environments. Description and illustration of each category of procedures follow.

Unstructured Interviews And Informal Direct Observation

Useful diagnostic information about the potential instigating and maintaining influences may be obtained initially (a) from unstructured written or verbal accounts provided by persons who have firsthand experience with the client and/or (b) through informal or unstructured direct observation of the person in the various situations in which SIBs occur. Persons providing the narrative accounts may include parents and other persons in the client's place of residence as well as staff in educational, vocational, therapy, recreational, and other program settings. Initial inquiry is guided by questions about the time, location, and personal/environmental contexts of the SIBs. During this inquiry, attention is focused on antecedents as well as the potential functions served by the SIBs. In addition, the variability of the SIBs under specific conditions, (e.g., "When I ask him to attend to his work") would be explored. To illustrate the potential value of this line of inquiry, it may be reported that self-injurious episodes appear more frequently following staff directives when the client is "in a bad mood" or "doesn't feel good." Such information would suggest an increased likelihood of SIBs when psychological and biomedical setting events are combined with staff directives.

These narrative accounts may be followed by or coincide with several informal or unstructured direct observations of the client in those situations in which SIBs are reported to occur. Information gained during these initial unstructured interviews and informal observations provides a basis for (a) formulating operational definitions of the target behaviors (b) and devising a more structured assessment format in which initial impressions concerning antecedents and subsequent events become specific items of formal inquiry. This may consists of a structured interview and/or a formalized direct observation format. A more structured format is useful as information obtained through an informal procedures may result in an overestimation of both the frequency and severity of self-injurious episodes.

Operational Definition of SIBs

The initial step in devising a structured assessment format to guide either interviews or direct observations involves developing operational definitions of the specific SIBs presented by an individual. This includes defining the type(s) as well as the range in severity of each. Table 6.1 includes examples of definitions of different types of SIBs.

Assessment of Severity of SIBs

A Self-Injury Trauma Scale (SIT) developed by Iwata et al. (1990b) provides a reliable method for collecting data on the severity of SIBs, viz., surface tissue damage caused by the self-injury. The SIT permits differentiation of self-injurious behaviors according to:

- **Type of self injury**, e.g., biting; eye gouging; picking skin;

- **Location of the injury** on the body, e.g., ear; face; back; foot/toe;

- **Type of injury**, i.e., abrasion or laceration; contusion;

- **Number of injuries**, i.e., range from 0 to 17 or more; and

- **Estimate of severity,** e.g., area is red; local swelling only; deep break in skin; tissue rupture.

These assessment data are summarized and used to provide an

TABLE 6.1 Definitions of Self-Injurious Behaviors*

Behavior	Definition
Eye gouging	• Any contact of any part of hand within the ocular area.
Face slapping	• Hitting face with palm of open hand in a forceful manner.
	• Forceful contact of the open hand with the face.
Hair pulling	• Closure of the fingers and thumb on hair with a pulling motion away from the head.
Hand mouthing	• Insertion of one or more fingers into the mouth.
Head banging	• Hitting head on an object (e.g., table top, floor, wall).
	• Forceful contact of the head with stationary environmental object.
Head hitting	• Hits face with fist with such force that head is moved as a consequence of the hit.
	• Strikes right temple with hand forcefully.
Self-pinching	• Places thumb and forefinger of right hand over skin of left arm and raises skin (pinches).

*Sources: Day et al. (1988); Durand and Carr (1001); Iwata et al. (1982).

estimate of current risk (low to high) based on location and severity of the injuries. While not typically used to provide functional analysis information, the SIT does represent a potentially useful means of providing preintervention baseline data on severity of SIBs. Additionally, the SIT may be used after intervention has begun as a means of substantiating changes in severity associated with successful intervention. It is not unusual to observe initial reduction in severity of SIBs prior to a noticeable decrease in frequency of the self-injury.

Rating Scales

The **Motivational Assessment Scale** (MAS) developed by Durand and Crimmins (1988) represents a useful assessment procedure for identifying the potential motivational determinants of self-injurious behavior. The MAS is a 16-item questionnaire that evaluates the client's SIBs in four types of situations reflecting possible maintaining variables: (a) **decreased adult attention**, (e.g., Does this behavior occur whenever you stop attending to him or her?), (b) **increased academic demands**, (e.g., Does this behavior occur following a command to perform a difficult task?), (c) **restricted access to tangibles**, (e.g., Does this behavior ever occur to get a toy, food, or game that he or she has been told that he or she can't have?), and (d) **unstructured settings**, (e.g., When this behavior is occurring, does your child seem unaware of anything else going on around him or her?). Four items representative of conditions in each of the four areas are presented as questions and rated from 0 (Never) to 6 (Always) by a person who has close contact with the person exhibiting the problem behavior. It is suggested that the MAS can be completed in 5 to 10 minutes. Total scores in each of the categories of attention, escape, tangibles, and sensory feedback provides a description of the relative influence of each. Durand and Cummins (1988), Durand et al. (1989), and Durand and Kishi (1987) report use of the MAS in devising effective intervention programs.

Structured Interviews

A functional analysis structured interview format described by O'Neill et al. (1990), while not designed specifically for self-injury, is nonetheless quite applicable. This **Functional Analysis Interview** includes the following sections:

A. **Behavior Description.** For each target behavior of concern, information is requested concerning its topography, frequency, duration, and intensity. Additionally, the informant is asked to identify and describe behaviors that occur together, i.e., at the same time; in a predictable sequence or chain, or in response to the same situation.

B. **Potential Ecological Events that May Affect Behavior(s).** Information is obtained concerning such topics as the (a) medications taken by the client and an impression about how these may affect the client's behavior, (b) medical complications (e.g., seizures, asthma, allergies) experienced by the person and an impression of how these may affect the person's target behavior(s), (c) sleep cycles of the person and how these may affect the person's target behaviors, (d) eating routines and diet and how these may affect the target behaviors, (e) typical daily schedule of activities and the predictability for the person of these, (e) frequency with which the person is provided an opportunity to make choices about daily activities, reinforcers, and the like, (f) variety of activities performed daily, and (g) other such variables as the potential effects of density of people, staffing pattern, and the nature of the task/activities presented during the day.

C. **Conditions That Predict Occurrence of the Behavior(s).** Inquiry is made about conditions that are most and least likely to correlate with the target behavior including time of day, setting, persons, activities, and other events listed by the informant.

D. **Maintaining Consequences/Functions of the Behavior(s).** The informant is asked to describe (a) what the person gets and/or avoids by engaging in each of the target behaviors and (b) the influence on the target behavior of such conditions as task difficulty, interruption of a desired event, presentation of a command or reprimand, being ignored for 15 minutes, changes in routine, and being alone.

E. **The Efficiency of the Behavior(s).** Information is obtained regarding the physical effort involved in the target behavior, the frequency with which the target behavior gains reinforcement, and the delay between the behavior and a consequence.

F. **Primary Method(s) of Communication.** Information is obtained about the type and level of complexity of the person's expressive and receptive communication skills.

G. **Reinforcing Events.** The informant describes events, activities, objects, and people that appear to serve as reinforcers for the person.

H. **Functional Alternative Behaviors.** Prosocial behaviors are described that may be used by the person as means of obtaining the same consequences that follow the SIBs and other target behaviors. Additionally, the informant describes teaching methods that are most likely to result in a positive teaching session along with those methods that would interfere with teaching.

I. **History of the Target Behavior(s), Previous Programs and Effects.** The structured interview is closed with the informant describing the history of the target behaviors, previous program approaches used and the effects of these.

Information gained from the structured interview is summarized in a Functional Analysis Interview Summary Form (O'Neill, 1990). In some instances, analysis of this information may be useful in developing an integrated set of diagnostic-intervention formulations. In most instances of chronic and multiply influenced SIBs, however, the information gained from this structured interview would be used to develop a structured format to guide direct observations of the person in the context of both high-risk and low-risk conditions.

Structured Direct Observation

Direct observation of the person in those natural settings in which SIBs occur represents an additional, and frequently a necessary, means of gaining functional diagnostic information. Direct observation guided by a structured format provides a means of confirmation and clarification of information obtained during structured interviews or questionnaire procedures. Carr et al. (1994) suggest that extensive direct observation may be valuable in ruling out an overshadowing effect in which severe problems are mentioned at the expense of not reporting other problems that, although of less severity, may nonetheless require intervention. Further, a person's negative reactions to certain situations may have caused intervention agents to avoid these situations. Prolonged observations, however, may provide demonstration of these situations and the resulting problem behavior. Additionally, direct observation may reveal any discrepancy between what an intervention agent reports about how they respond to specific aberrant behaviors and how they may actually respond. Finally, direct observation is valuable in verifying that a problem behavior is indeed socially mediated rather than being either self-stimulatory in nature or maintained by its physical effect on the environment independent of a social mediator. This discrimination becomes critical in devising interventions based on maintaining influences.

Carr et al. (1994) describe a procedure for obtaining observational data. An index card is used by an observer to record each incident of the target behavior as it occurs. The observer records the **date and time of occurrence**, **general context** (e.g., lunch, gym), **interpersonal context** (e.g., Teacher talking to another adult. Child and peers sitting at a table.), **problem behavior** (e.g., Tom began yelling and hitting self in face.), and **social reaction** (e.g., Staff member guided his hand to his side and talked softly to him.). In using a similar procedure, we have found an additional **comments** section to be useful in suggesting potential secondary instigating conditions. In this modified format, the observer is directed to describe any additional environmental or personal conditions that appear to influence the person's target behaviors.

Following a 2-week observation period, the resulting index cards are sorted into categories based on the type of antecedent environmental conditions and on the presumed consequences produced. In this manner, (a) descriptions are obtained of various antecedent conditions following which self-injury is most likely to occur and (b) hypotheses are developed about the motivational basis for the person's aberrant behaviors. This analysis provides one or more testable hypotheses relating to both instigating conditions and maintaining variables.

In this analysis, it is not unusual to find that self-injury of a person is multiply motivated, that is, motivated at various times by such different consequences as social feedback, escape from aversive conditions, and acquisition of specific tangibles. In frequent instances, as demonstrated by a number of functional analysis studies, a predominate source of motivation typically becomes evident for an individual, with other conditions assuming less significance as sources of impetus for a person's SIBs (Carr & Durand, 1985; Carr et al., in press; Smith et al., 1993). The resulting motivational hierarchy, in illustration, may identify escape as being of most significance, with social feedback of less significance.

In frequent instances, a specific motivational condition will be associated with multiple instigating conditions. In illustration, a person's escape-motivated SIBs may be associated with such different instigating conditions as instructional demands, taunts from peers, an intense state of dysphoria, and physical pain. As depicted in Figure 6.2, description of each of these instigating conditions is valuable as each provides direction to specific intervention formulations. Treatment or management for SIBs motivated by escape under conditions of instructional demands may differ significantly from that provided escape-motivated SIBs under the instigating conditions of physical pain or an intense state of dysphoria.

Mace et al. (1992) and O'Neill et al. (1990) describe alternative structured direct observation procedures. Each is provided brief description to acquaint the reader with alternative descriptive analytic systems.

Unstructured narrative accounts of a person's target behavior and the environmental events that surround its occurrence are used by Mace et al. (1992) to identify 3-5 categories each of antecedent and subsequent events that cooccur naturally with the behavior. As illustrated by the writers, self-injury of a client may include hand-biting and head banging. Antecedents may consist of task demands, social interaction, and others present-no interaction. Subsequent events may be consoling comments, reprimands, and discontinuation of task preferences.

Data on these SIBs and related antecedent and subsequent event categories are collected using a direct observation continuous 10-second partial-interval recording procedure. Antecedent events are recorded on each occurrence throughout the observation session. On occurrence of a target behavior, the observer records it along with the events in the subsequent categories for the next two 10-second intervals. Observation sessions should be of sufficient length to observe several occurrences of self-injury in each session.

Observational data obtained from individual sessions are grouped and summarized as conditional probabilities of the form "Given the occurrence of a particular antecedent event, what is the probability of observing a contiguous self-injurious response?" Additionally, these data provide a basis for formulating hypotheses about maintaining conditions. This descriptive analytic process, as emphasized by the writers, provides only correlational data and does not demonstrate causal relationships. The manner of increasing confidence in these descriptive data is discussed in the following section on analogue assessment.

O'Neill et al. (1990) provide a final example of a useful descriptive analysis procedure. A Functional Analysis Observation Form makes use of an event recording procedure in which entries are made on the recording form at the time the target behavior occurs. The Observation Form directs the observer to record within specified time periods the occurrence of client-specific target behaviors, the correlated setting events/discriminative stimuli, the perceived functions served by the behavior, the actual consequences, and other data as deemed relevant. The authors recommend data collection across as many settings and during as much time per day as is clinically feasible. The resulting information identifies where and when the problem behaviors both **do** and **do not** occur. It is recommended that data be collected for a minimum of 2-5 days or until a minimum of 10-15 occurrences of the behavior have been recorded. Additional data may be required depending upon the presence of patterns of antecedents-behavior-consequences that evolve.

These observational data are summarized in a Functional Analysis Observation Summary Form that highlights possible antecedent-behavior consequence relationships. These provide the basis for developing related interventions.

Beyond Descriptive Analysis

Descriptive analysis results in a set of hypotheses about the instigating and maintaining variables associated with the occurrence of SIBs. At this stage, the clinician may seek to obtain verification for these presumed relationships by means of a controlled or experimental analysis. This verification phase may consist of direct manipulation of the hypothesized controlling conditions either in the person's natural settings or under more controlled analogue conditions.

Carr et al. (in press) provides an example of the natural setting analysis. Following identification of conditions that serve as antecedents to aberrant behaviors presumed to reflect the influence of specific motivational conditions (e.g., social attention), several scenarios are constructed to reflect each. In illustration, assume that a person's SIBs serve the purpose of gaining staff attention when they are interacting with others. Scenarios may be constructed that would involve staff assisting another child with a table task, talking with others about an upcoming event, and demonstrating to another child how to operate a vending machine. After developing a variety of scenarios depicting the range of identified instigating and related maintaining variables, the final step in this analysis involves exposing the person to the array of scenarios. Each is presented several times a day for several days across a number of settings and persons. If target problem behaviors occur consistently under the various scenario conditions and infrequently or never when these conditions are not present, it can be concluded with some assurance that these conditions are causal in producing these behaviors. Specific intervention strategies can then be designed to address these scenario conditions.

Analogue Assessment

A second procedure for identifying the functional properties of self-injury on a pre treatment basis is the analogue assessment. This functional analysis is based on the work of Iwata et al. (1982), Carr and Durand (1985), and Durand and Carr (1987). An analogue condition is a contrived situation that simulates environmental circumstances present in the client's natural environment. In this procedure, specific instigating and maintaining variables suspected to influence the SIBs of an individual are systematically applied and withdrawn under controlled analogue conditions provided in a setting separate from the person's natural environment. The client typically is exposed to each simulated condition during 10- to 15-minute sessions. These are repeated until patterns of co-variations are discerned. As examples of the time required for this analogue assessment, Day et al. (1988), exposed a child to four different simulated conditions repeated three or four times a day for a minimum of three days. Wacker et al. (1990) used three to five assessments for each of four simulated conditions, with each session lasting between 6 to 10 minutes.

Analogue assessments described in the behavior analysis literature typically include simulated conditions reflecting **positive reinforcement** (SIBs result in attention or tangible), **negative reinforcement** (SIBs result in escape from the instigating condition, typically a task demand), and **sensory-input alone** (SIBs result in no contingent consequences for appropriate or self-injurious behaviors). Studies have described variations of the following:

Attention Condition. This condition is designed to simulate a positive reinforcement contingency involving social attention often observed to occur in the natural environment, especially in institutional settings with low staff-to-client ratios. In these settings, SIBs often produce considerable concern and attention from staff and other behaviors receiving relatively less feedback.

As a simulation of this condition, a therapist and client are together in a room with a variety of toys within easy reach of the client. The client is directed to play with the toys while the therapist "does some work," e.g., the therapist sits in a chair across the room and begins reading a book or magazine. Contingent on each episode of self-injury, statements of concern and disapproval are provided (e.g., Don't do that, you're going to hurt yourself.) and paired with brief physical contact such as touching the client's shoulder or interrupting the self-injurious response. All other behaviors of the client are ignored (Iwata et al., 1990).

In a variation of this condition designed to evaluate positive reinforcement involving tangible consequences, a teacher, a child presenting SIBs, and a small number of peers are observed in a room containing items or activities previously identified as preferred by the target child (Day et al., 1988). The session begins with the teacher offering these items to the peers. If the target child exhibits SIBs, the teacher provides the child access to the activity, object, or edible being offered the peers. Free access to these preferred events are provided for 20-30 seconds, at which time the reinforcing event is terminated and the sequence repeated.

Demand/Escape Condition. This condition assesses the effects on SIBs of contingent escape from or avoidance of an instructional or other task sequence. If SIBs are responsive to this contingency, a negative reinforcement function is demonstrated.

In illustration of this simulation, educational or work tasks are presented to a client seated at a desk or table. The occurrence of SIBs results in a time-out from task demands. Following removal of tasks for a short period, e.g., 15-30 seconds, the sequence is repeated (Day et al.; Wacker et al., 1990).

In a variation of this negative reinforcement simulation, Iwata et al. (1990) noted during informal observations that a child's SIBs were most likely to occur in response to medical examination and questioning about his numerous physical handicaps. A simulated medical examination was devised to evaluate the hypothesis that SIBs were being maintained by escape from these conditions. During the simulated examination, periodic praise was provided for compliance. Contingent on SIBs, the simulated examination was interrupted as in the Demand conditions described above. After a short elapse of time, the examination was continued.

Alone Condition. This condition is designed to evaluate sensory-input as the maintaining variable. SIBs occurring when in this condition may represent a means of obtaining sensory stimulation.

In simulating this "barren environment" condition that is devoid of sources of social or physical stimulation, the client is placed in a room alone or in a vacant desk in a vacant part of a classroom without access to materials that may serve as external sources of stimulation. No social consequences follow occurrence of SIBs.

When SIBs are observed to co-vary reliably with specific stimulus conditions in the controlled analogue setting, these functional relationships are used as a basis for selecting related interventions for use in the person's natural environment.

Developing Interventions Based On Functional Diagnostics

We have found it valuable in working with professional staff in residential and community programs to use the Multimodal Functional Diagnostics Worksheet (Figure 6.2) and the Specific Discipline Diagnostic-Intervention Formulations Worksheet (Figure 6.3) to guide the assessment process and to insure a close interface between diagnostic formulations and associated interventions. With these worksheets as guides, various staff organize their impressions about a client prior to an initial staffing. During this initial meeting, each person in attendance is prepared to discuss the potential and relative influences of a variety of instigating and maintaining conditions. As noted in Figure 6.2, each staff member from his or her own professional perspective is guided to consider a variety of potential environmental and personal instigating and maintaining influences. Results of these initial assessments are summarized in the format depicted in Figure 6.3. During the staffing, the clinicians describe their initial set of diagnostic-intervention formulations (Columns A and B, Figure 6.3). As examples, if Mr. Foy is observed to engage in SIBs when requested to attend a large group program, provide a similar experience but in a small group. Follow this management procedure with treatment to reduce the aversive features of large groups through gradual exposure to programs involving an increasingly larger number of peers. If Miss Dean uses SIBs as a means of insuring staff intervention when a peer becomes pesky, teach her an alternative functionally equivalent means of gaining staff assistance. If Miss Curran's SIBs coincide with periods of depression, treat this emotional disorder as a means of reducing or removing the setting influence of the distressful dysphoric affective state.

These are supported or deleted based on information offered by other staff. This initial meeting ends with a plan for obtaining more formal diagnostic information. In illustration, a formal psychiatric evaluation may be undertaken to ascertain the presence of a mental disorder as a potential source of influence. A neurological consult may be undertaken to evaluate the question of undetected seizure activity that had been suggested as a possible secondary (setting) influence on the SIBs. A formal direct observation format may be devised as a means of gathering Antecedent-Behavior-Consequence data during designated high- and low-risk time periods.

In subsequent meetings, data obtained from these various additional assessment procedures, including structured direct observation, are used to support or modify initial diagnostic formulations. The final product of the multidisciplinary assessment efforts is the development of the Multimodal Integrated Intervention Plan as depicted previously in Figure 6.1. This combined set of diagnostic intervention formulations and related implementation actions becomes the current working MIIP. During routinely scheduled reviews of data associated with interventions, the Plan is modified as needed to reflect these effects.

Summary

Multimodal functional diagnostics provide the basis for development of a MIIP that reflects the contributions of various professional disciplines. Each intervention is diagnostically based and addresses primary and secondary instigating and related maintaining conditions and relevant tertiary vulnerability factors hypothesized to be associated with a person's SIBs. The effects of interventions are evaluated through results obtained from the intervention-specific data monitoring procedures. Modifications in the Plan are made as needed to insure successful attainment of objectives.

Chapters 7 and 8 present description of a range of specific biomedical and psychosocial interventions for self-injury.

SEVEN

Clinical Applications: Biomedical Treatment Paradigms

Introduction

As noted in Chapter 3, there is no single specific biomedical treatment for SIBs. Rather, interventions may address a variety of conditions presumed to contribute to the occurrence of SIBs. As with psychosocial approaches, biological interventions should be based on hypotheses about potential contributing conditions. In some few instances, biomedical intervention may address conditions assumed to play a primary role in producing SIBs. As illustrated previously, conditions such as mental illness, adverse drug effects, seizure disorders, and specific illnesses such as a migraine headache may represent the necessary and sufficient conditions that occasion SIBs. Biomedical interventions in these instances may significantly reduce or eliminate the SIBs.

In frequent instances, however, biomedical factors represent significant **contributing** (secondary or setting) but not **sufficient** conditions resulting in the occurrence of SIBs. As noted earlier, these secondary influences are illustrated by a generalized biologically-based irritability and the distress accompanying menses or a toothache. Biomedical interventions in these instances address the various setting event conditions that render the person at risk to engage in SIBs when confronted with other primary instigating conditions such as a directive to engage in a nonpreferred activity or a taunt from a peer. Following removal or reduction in the biomedical states, the person is less likely to engage in SIBs when again confronted with these or similar psychosocial conditions. These biomedical interventions are closely interfaced with psychosocial interventions designed to teach the person alternative means of coping with the combined biomedical and psychosocial stimulus complex.

Historically, drug therapy has been used in a nonspecific manner in an attempt to decrease or eliminate SIBs without consideration of the conditions which were instigating and maintaining the behavior. Medication was empirically prescribed with the expectation that positive drug effects would overcome whatever conditions were mediating the SIBs. In general, this meant the indiscriminate use of antipsychotic agents, often with the mistaken assumption that the client was suffering from a psychotic illness.

Use of psychotropic drug therapy for SIBs can now be based on a more rational consideration of (a) the complex of behaviors, psychological symptoms, and physical signs which indicate that the client has a problem that is responsive to biological therapies and (b) factors that predict response to specific agents. Although prescribing psychotropic agents remains an inexact science, it is now possible to make informed and integrated choices based upon specific hypotheses.

Therapeutic Treatment Paradigms

Before implementing a course of psychotropic drug therapy for persons with developmental disabilities who have SIBs, it is important to have developed a rationale for treatment which includes a consideration of how drug therapy might modify the conditions influencing the target behavior as well as a diagnostic hypothesis. Using a "paradigm approach" to treatment is essential because it provides a clinically relevant method for selecting specific agents based upon mechanisms-of-action rather than on an empirical basis of simply matching a behavior with a drug. In addition, it provides a blueprint for selecting subsequent therapies, should the first medication prescribed be ineffective or the client develop significant adverse reactions to it. In general, there are five paradigms for using psychotropic drug therapy.

Paradigm 1: Psychiatric Syndrome

In this paradigm, drug-responsive maladaptive behavior is considered to be a mental illness epiphenomenon. The choice of specific treatments is based upon the treatment of the mental illness itself, not the behavior. In other words, the self- injury is a second order behavior that represents an individual's adaptation to having a mental illness. If it can be established that the individual is suffering from a drug-responsive psychiatric disorder such as major depression and that the maladaptive behavior is functionally linked to the illness, treatment is directed towards the mental illness. Thus, the treatment of depression-associated SIBs, for example, is antidepressant therapy and the first order behaviors and symptoms of the depression are the primary treatment targets.

William Bazemore, a 45-year-old man with severe disabilities, was referred for a psychiatric assess-ment of SIBs which had been present for at least 20 years. Mr. Bazemore would head bang several times per day, if not wearing a helmet. He frequently required one-to-one supervision and had not re-sponded to a variety of positive psychosocial inter-ventions. In the past, aversive interventions had been unsucessfully tried (e.g., ammonia, water mist) and he had not responded to antipsychotic drug therapy, beta blocker therapy with propranolol (Inderal), or opiate antagonist therapy with naltrexone (Trexan). A psychiatric consultant noted that in addition to SIBs, Mr. Bazemore would intermittently cry, never smiled, did not seem to enjoy age and developmental level appropriate activities, and his sleep was inter-rupted. Based upon a provisional diagnosis of chronic major depression, sertraline (Zoloft) therapy was initiated. After 30 days, his SIBs had stopped and he was observed to repeatedly smile and request spe-cific activities and objects. Objective data tracking of his sleep indicated that he was now sleeping through-out the night.

Paradigm 2: Neuropsychiatric

In this paradigm, drug-responsive maladaptive behavior represents a disruption of primary neurobiological functional processes.

Mary Devito is a 23-year-old woman with congenital rubella and severe disabilities, who lives with three roommates in a staffed apartment. Her behavior has begun to jeopardize her living arrangements. Since early childhood, Ms. Devito has had severe overactivity, often sleeping during the day and remaining awake at night, and engaging in severe face slapping when frustrated. Her overactivity, disordered sleep-wake cycles, and low frustration tolerance were considered to be first order behavior reflecting CNS dysfunction, and carbamazepine (Tegretol) therapy was initiated. When a steady-state carbamazepine blood level of 9.0 mg/L was achieved, her sleep normalized, her activity level decreased, and she now face slaps less than once per month.

Of particular importance in this paradigm is the management of arousal, irritability, and rage, all of which can occur in the presence of brain dysfunction. Overarousal, for example, may respond to beta blocker therapy, clonidine, or buspirone. Irritability may respond to serotonergic antidepressants, carbamazepine, or lithium.

Paradigm 3: Psychological Distress

Some drug-responsive maladaptive behavior represents an attempt to modulate a nonspecific negative mood state. Anticipatory anxiety in the absence of a specific psychiatric disorder or CNS disturbance would be an example.

John Seymore is a 23-year-old man with mild impairments who had decided to attend a 3-week summer
camp for young adults with developmental disabilities. This would be his first experience living away
from his parents. After being told on June 1st that he
would attend the camp's first session beginning July
1st, he became acutely agitated. He would
perseveratively ask his parents and vocational coun-
selors about whether his job would be available when
he returned from vacation, he developed disturbed
sleep, and was noted to be easily startled and, when
frustrated, would face slap. He was started on
diazepam (Valium) 5 mg twice per day for the remaining three weeks prior to going to camp. His symptoms
remitted and the drug was discontinued on the day
after his arrival at camp.

Paradigm 4: Neurological

In this paradigm, drug-responsive maladaptive behaviors represent involuntary motor or affective discharges unrelated to external
events. A neurological model is implicit in the **DSM-III-R** diagnosis of
intermittent explosive disorder. (The **DSM-III-R** notes that the existence
of this disorder is doubted by many clinicians [APA, 1987].)

In clinical practice, neurologic-based behavior seems quite rare
and drug therapy based upon a neurological paradigm should be
reserved for cases in which behavior is associated with clearcut seizure
activity.

Paradigm 5: Learned Behavior

Drug-responsive maladaptive behavior represents an attempt

to produce physiological positive reinforcement. This paradigm has been used to explain the response of SIBs to opiate antagonists such as naltrexone (Trexan) (Sandman, 1990/1991), especially in persons with autism in which there are alterations in CNS beta-endorphin activity, a naturally occurring opiate-like neurotransmitter/modulator (Hermann, 1991; Sandman, 1990/1991).

Treatment Principles

When drug therapy of SIBs is being considered, the following treatment principles should be followed in a stepwise manner.

 Conduct an adequate functional diagnostic assessment as a basis for isolating potential contributors to the self-injury.

There is no specific drug therapy for SIBs, but there may be one for an underlying neuropsychiatric disturbance.

 Hypothesize a mechanism of action for the way in which the alteration in function is manifest as self-injury.

Developing an explanation of the way in which an identified CNS functional deficit or psychiatric disorder presents as self-injury helps in drug selection (matching a drug effect with the identified dysfunction) and the determination of outcome measures.

 Select a pharmacological agent which is directed to the primary cause of the problem.

There should be some evidence that the selected drug be efficacious for the problem being treated. In addition, factors such as impact on cognitive function, interactions with pre-existing physical illnesses and co-prescribed medications should be considered.

 Specify what will constitute a therapeutic trial of the selected drug.

The parameters of a therapeutic trial should be stated prior to the onset of treatment. This should include the duration of therapy at a specified maximum therapeutic daily dose or blood level.

 Start treatment only after an objective behavior monitoring system is in place.

The purpose of the objective monitoring system is to provide a way of determining drug effects without relying on the subjective impressions of individual caregivers. The system will be helpful in assessing not only claims of efficacy, but also those in which it is claimed that the client is worse.

It is critical that the measures to be tracked are consistent with what can be expected with drug therapy. In some cases, the expected outcome is a decrease in frequency of the SIBs, especially when they represent a generalized adaptive response that is being exacerbated by a psychiatric disorder. In addition, measures not directly related to behavior, e.g., a sleep disturbance, may be helpful in determining medication response.

 Decide in advance what will constitute a positive treatment response.

In some cases, it is to be expected that the SIBs will **completely remit** with drug therapy. This would be the case when the behavior represents a state-dependent phenomenon as an episodic illness such as bipolar disorder. In other cases, SIBs may represent a second-order behavior, the frequency/severity of which is only partially related to the psychiatric disorder being treated. The overarousal associated with fragile X syndrome may, for example, produce stress-induced face slapping that increases in severity when the affected individual develops a depressive disorder (Tranebjaerg & Orum, 1991). Thus, treating the depression will result in a decrease in the rate and severity of SIBs, but it will not completely remit because the stressors of every day life may still provoke it.

Drug Selection Principles

Drug therapies for specific psychiatric disorders and symptom/ behavior complexes are listed in Tables 7.1 through 7.4. A Drug Brand Name Glossary is included in Table 7.5. There is an extensive research data base regarding the pharmacological treatment of classic psychiatric syndromes. This database can be utilized in treatment decision-making because it is the presence of syndrome-specific features that determines the type of drug therapy to select, irrespective of whether or not the individual presents a developmental disability.

TABLE 7.1 TREATMENT OPTIONS FOR MOOD DISORDERS

major depression	• tricyclic antidepressants e.g., amitriptyline, amoxapine, desipramine, doxepin, imipramine, nortriptyline, protriptyline
	• monoamine oxidase inhibitors, e.g., isocarboxazid, phenelzine, tranylcypromine
	• serotonin selective reuptake inhibitors (SSRIs), e.g., fluoxetine, paroxetine, sertraline
	• other antidepressants, e.g., trazodone, bupropion

TABLE 7.1 TREATMENT OPTIONS FOR MOOD DISORDERS (continued)

acute mania	<ul><li>lithium</li><li>carbamazepine</li><li>valproate</li><li>benzodiazepines, e.g., clonazepam and lorazepam</li><li>antipsychotics, e.g., haloperidol</li><li>verapamil</li></ul>
bipolar disorder, maintenance therapy	<ul><li>lithium</li><li>carbamazepine</li><li>valproate</li><li>verapamil</li></ul>

TABLE 7.2 TREATMENT OPTIONS FOR ANXIETY DISORDERS

generalized anxiety disorder	<ul><li>benzodiazepines, e.g., alprazolam, chlordiazepoxide, diazepam, lorazepam, oxazepam</li><li>buspirone</li><li>beta blockers, e.g., nadolol, propranolol</li><li>clonidine</li></ul>
obsessive-compulsive disorder	<ul><li>SSRIs</li><li>clomipramine</li></ul>
panic disorder	<ul><li>benzodiazepines alprazolam, clonazepam</li><li>tricyclic antidepressants, e.g., desipramine</li><li>SSRIs</li><li>MAOIs</li></ul>

(continued)

TABLE 7.2 TREATMENT OPTIONS FOR ANXIETY DISORDERS (continued)

| post-traumatic stress disorder | Target of treatment is an associated symptom complex such as anxiety or depression. |

TABLE 7.3 TREATMENT OPTIONS FOR PSYCHOTIC DISORDERS

schizophrenia	• antipsychotics, e.g., chlorpromazine, clozapine, haloperidol, mesoridazine, thioridazine, trifluoperazine
schizoaffective disorder	• antipsychotics + mood disorder therapy (see Table 6.1)
atypical psychosis	• antipsychotics

TABLE 7.4 TREATMENT OPTIONS FOR OTHER PSYCHIATRIC DISORDERS

| attention deficit disorder | • stimulants, e.g., dextroamphetamine, methylphenidate, pemoline |

TABLE 7.4 TREATMENT OPTIONS FOR OTHER PSYCHIATRIC DISORDERS (continued)

	• tricyclic antidepressants, e.g., desipramine • buproprion • clonidine
Tourette disorder	• antipsychotics, e.g., haloperidol, pimozide • verapamil • clonidine

Symptoms and behaviors associated with organic mental disorders

rage attacks	• propranolol
overactivity	• lithium • carbamazepine • valproate
irritability	• SSRIs • carbamazepine • lithium
arousal	• beta blockers, e.g., nadolol, propranolol • buspirone • clonidine
hallucinations and delusions	• antipsychotics
stereotypic SIBs	• opiate antagonists • antipsychotics

TABLE 7.5 DRUGS USED TO TREAT PSYCHIATRIC DISOR-
DERS: A GENERIC NAME - BRAND NAME GLOSSARY[a]

acetophenazine	Tindal[b] (antipsychotic)
Adapin	doxepin
alprazolam	Xanax (benzodiazepine)
amantadine	Symmetrel (antiparkinson)
amitriptyline	Elavil (tricyclic antidepressant)
amobarbital	Amytal (barbiturate)
amoxapine	Asendin (tricyclic antidepressant)
Amytal, sodium	amobarbital
Anafranil	clomipramine
Antabuse	disulfiram
Artane	trihexyphenidyl
Asendin	amoxapine
Atarax	hydroxyzine
Ativan	lorazepam
Aventyl	nortriptyline
Benadryl	diphenhydramine
benztropine	Cogentin (antiparkinson)
bethanechol	Urecholine (cholinergic)
bupropion	Wellbutrin (antidepressant)
Buspar	buspirone (antianxiety)
buspirone	Buspar
Calan	verapamil (calcium channel blocker)

a The listed drugs include those with psychotropic properties irrespective of whether they are classified as psychotropic agents, e.g.,
clonidine (Catapres) is a hypertensive drug with antianxiety properties. Drug class listed in parentheses for generic drug name.
b The first letters of drug brand names are capitalized. Only the most
representative brand name or names are listed. There may be
others as well.
c This is the Canadian brand name.
d Drug is available in Canada, but not in the United States.

TABLE 7.5 DRUGS USED TO TREAT PSYCHIATRIC DISORDERS: A GENERIC NAME - BRAND NAME GLOSSARY (continued)

carbamazepine	Tegretol (anticonvulsant)
Catapres	clonidine
Centrax	prazepam
chloral hydrate	Noctec (sedative)
chlordiazepoxide	Librium (benzodiazepine)
chlorpromazine	Thorazine, Largactil^c (antipsychotic)
chlorprothixene	Taractan (antipsychotic)
clobazam^d	Frisium (benzodiazepine)
clomipramine	Anafranil (tricyclic antidepressant)
clonazepam	Klonopin, Rivotril^c (benzodiazepine)
clonidine	Catapres (anti-adrenergic)
clorazepate	Tranxene (benzodiazepine)
Cogentin	benztropine
Compazine	prochlorperazine
Corgard	nadolol
Cylert	pemoline
cyproheptadine	Periactin (antihistamine)
Dalmane	flurazepam
Delsym	dextromethorphan
Depakene	valproic acid, valproate
Depakote	divalproex sodium
Deprol	meprobamate + benactyzine
desipramine	Norpramin, Pertofrane (tricyclic antidepressant)
Desyrel	trazodone
Dexedrine	dextroamphetamine
dextroamphetamine	Dexedrine (stimulant)
dextromethorphan	Delsym (serotonergic)
diazepam	Valium (benzodiazepine)
Dilantin	phenytoin
diphenhydramine	Benadryl (antihistamine)
disulfiram	Antabuse (antialcoholic)

(continued)

**TABLE 7.5 DRUGS USED TO TREAT PSYCHIATRIC DISOR-
DERS: A GENERIC NAME - BRAND NAME GLOSSARY
(continued)**

divalproex sodium	Depakote (anticonvulsant)
Doral	quazepam (benzodiazepine)
doxepin	Adapin, Sinequan (tricyclic antidepressant)
droperidol	Inapsine (antipsychotic)
Elavil	amitriptyline
Eldepryl	selegiline
Eskalith	lithium (antimanic)
estazolam	Prosom (benzodiazepine)
Etrafon	amitriptyline + perphenazine
Fluanxol	fluphenthixol[d]
Fluanxol Depot	fluphenthixol decanoate
fluoxetine	Prozac (SSRI antidepressant)
fluphenazine	Prolixin (antipsychotic)
fluphenazine decanoate	Prolixin Decanoate, Modecate[c]
fluphenazine enanthate	Prolixin Enanthate, Moditen Enanthate[c]
fluphenthixol[d]	Fluanxol (antipsychotic)
fluphenthixol decanoate	Fluanxol Depot
flurazepam	Dalmane (benzodiazepine)
fluspiriline[d]	Imap (antipsychotic)
fluvoxamine[d]	Luvox (SSRI antidepressant)
Frisium	clobazam[d]
halazepam	Paxipam (benzodiazepine)
Halcion	triazolam
Haldol	haloperidol
haloperidol	Haldol (antipsychotic)
hydroxyzine	Atarax, Vistaril (antihistamine)
Imap	fluspiriline[d]
imipramine	Tofranil (tricyclic antidepressant)
Inapsine	droperidol
Inderal	propranolol
isocarboxazid	Marplan (MAOI antidepressant)

TABLE 7.5 DRUGS USED TO TREAT PSYCHIATRIC DISORDERS: A GENERIC NAME - BRAND NAME GLOSSARY (continued)

Isoptin	verapamil
ketazolam[d]	Loftran (benzodiazepine)
Klonopin	clonazepam
Largactil[c]	chlorpromazine
Librium	chlordiazepoxide
Levoprome	methotrimeprazine
levopromeprazine[d]	see methotrimeprazine
Limbitrol	amitriptyline + chlordiazepoxide
Lithane	lithium
lithium	Eskalith, Lithane (antimanic)
Loftran	ketazolam[d] (benzodiazepine)
lorazepam	Ativan (benzodiazepine)
loxapine	Loxitane (antipsychotic)
Loxitane	loxapine
Ludiomil	maprotiline
Luminal	phenobarbital
Luvox	fluvoxamine[d]
Majeptil	thioproperazine[d]
maprotiline	Ludiomil (cyclic antidepressant)
Marplan	isocarboxazid (MAOI-antidepressant)
Mebaral	mephobarbital
Mellaril	thioridazine
mephobarbital	Mebaral (barbiturate)
meprobamate	Miltown (antianxiety)
mesoridazine	Serentil (antipsychotic)
methotrimeprazine[d]	Nozinan, Levoprome (antipsychotic)
methylphenidate	Ritalin (stimulant)
Miltown	meprobamate
Moban	molindaone
Modecate[c]	fluphenazine decanoate
Moditen Enanthate[c]	fluphenazine enanthate
Mogadon	nitrazepam[d]
molindone	Moban (antipsychotic)
Mysoline	primidone

(continued)

**TABLE 7.5 DRUGS USED TO TREAT PSYCHIATRIC DISOR-
DERS: A GENERIC NAME - BRAND NAME GLOSSARY
(continued)**

nadolol	Corgard (beta blocker)
naltrexone	Narcan (opiate antagonist)
Narcan	naltrexone
Nardil	phenelzine (MAOI antidepressant)
Navane	thiothixene (antipsychotic)
nitrazepam[d]	Mogadon (benzodiazepine)
Noctec	chloral hydrate (sedative)
Norpramin	desipramine
nortriptyline	Aventyl, Pamelor (cyclic antidepressant)
Nozinan	methotrimeprazine[d]
Orap	pimozide (antipsychotic)
oxazepam	Serax (benzodiazepine)
Pamelor	nortriptyline
Paral	paraldehyde
paraldehyde	Paral (sedative)
Parnate	tranylcypromine
paroxetine	Paxil (SSRI antidepressant)
Paxil	paroxetine
Paxipam	halazepam (benzodiazepine)
pemoline	Cylert (stimulant)
Periactin	cyproheptadine
perphenazine	Trilafon (antipsychotic)
Pertofrane	desipramine
phenelzine	Nardil (MAOI antidepressant)
phenobarbital	Luminal (barbiturate)
phenytoin	Dilantin (anticonvulsant)
pimozide	Orap (antipsychotic)
pindolol	Visken (beta blocker)
prazepam	Centrax (benzodiazepine)
primidone	Mysoline (anticonvulsant)
prochlorperazine	Compazine (antipsychotic)
Prolixin	fluphenazine

TABLE 7.5 DRUGS USED TO TREAT PSYCHIATRIC DISORDERS: A GENERIC NAME - BRAND NAME GLOSSARY (continued)

promazine	Sparine (antipsychotic)
propranolol	Inderal (beta blocker)
Prosom	estazolam (benzodiazepine)
protriptyline	Vivactil (cyclic antidepressant)
Prozac	fluoxetine
quazepam	Doral (benzodiazepine)
reserpine	Serpasil (antipsychotic)
Restoril	temazepam (benzodiazepine)
Rivotril[c]	clonazepam
Ritalin	methylphenidate
selegiline	Eldepryl (MAOI antiparkinson)
Serax	oxazepam
Serentil	mesoridazine
Serpasil	reserpine
sertraline	Zoloft (SSRI antidepressant)
Sinequan	doxepin
Sparine	promazine
Stelazine	trifluoperazine
Surmontil	trimipramine
Symmetrel	amantadine
Taractan	chlorprothixine
temazepam	Restoril (benzodiazepine)
thioproperazine[d]	Majeptil (antipsychotic)
thioridazine	Mellaril (antipsychotic)
thiothixene	Navane (antipsychotic)
Thorazine	chlorpromazine
Tindal	acetophenazine
Tofranil	imipramine
Tranxene	clorazepate
tranylcypromine	Parnate (MAOI antidepressant)
trazodone	Desyrel (antidepressant)
Triavil	amitriptyline + perphenazine
triazolam	Halcion (benzodiazepine)

(continued)

TABLE 7.5 DRUGS USED TO TREAT PSYCHIATRIC DISOR-
DERS: A GENERIC NAME - BRAND NAME GLOSSARY
(continued)

trifluoperazine	Stelazine (antipsychotic)
trifluopromazine	Vesprin (antipsychotic)
trihexyphenidyl	Artane (antiparkinson)
Trilafon	perphenazine
trimipramine	Surmontil (tricyclic antidepressant)
Urecholine	bethanechol
Valium	diazepam
valproate	Depakene (anticonvulsant)
valproic acid	Depakene (anticonvulsant)
verapamil	Calan, Isoptin (calcium channel blocker)
Vesprin	trifluopromazine
Visken	pindolol
Vistaril	hydroxyzine
Wellbutrin	bupropion
Xanax	alprazolam
yohimbine	Yohimex (adrenergic)
Yohimex	yohimbine
Zoloft	sertraline

Treatment of Organic Mental Syndromes

With respect to the pharmacotherapy of organic mental syndromes, the lack of clearly defined diagnostic-drug formulations makes
the treatment of these disorders more empirical. Neurobiological
hypotheses of self-injury (Gedy, 1992; Sandman, 1990/1991) and
neuropharmacological mechanisms of action to explain drug effects
have been proposed (Gualtieri & Schroeder, 1989; Osman & Loschen,
1992), but validation remains problematic (Luchins, 1990).

The choice of a specific drug is further complicated by the fact that drugs from different pharmacological classes may produce similar effects (Luchin & Dolka, 1989). For example, a variety of drugs modulate serotonergic transmission (Stahl, 1992) and may have therapeutic effects in treating SIBs (Luchins, 1990; Markowitz, 1992; Miczek et al., 1989).

The relationship between specific symptoms and behaviors and drug response is further complicated because drugs such as carbamazepine (Tegretol) may be effective in a variety of different conditions, possibly by different mechanisms of action (Sovner, 1991). This may also be true for beta blockers such as propranolol (Inderal) that modulates both beta adrenergic and serotonergic activity (Glennon, 1990).

Use of Antipsychotic Agents

Antipsychotic (neuroleptic) drugs cannot be considered to be a treatment of first choice for SIBs associated with organic mental syndromes because they can cause disabling extrapyramidal reactions such as parkinsonian tremor and akathisia as well as potentially irreversible tardive dyskinesia. Low dose therapy seems most indicated in cases of stereotypic SIBs (Mikkelson, 1986).

Use of Narcotic Antagonists

The use of narcotic antagonists such as naltrexone (Trexan) to treat self-injury remains controversial and clearcut response-predictors have not been found (Sandman, 1990/1991). Naltrexone response appears to be related to the presence of high rates of SIBs in individuals with autism (Sandman, 1990/1991). Furthermore, opiates modulate serotonergic, dopaminergic and noradrenergic neurotransmission (Jaffe & Martin, 1990) so that it is unclear whether opiate antagonists act directly or indirectly in treating SIBs.

Other Factors in Drug Selection

In addition to the disorder or symptom/behavior complex being treated, the choice of a specific psychotropic agent requires a consideration of other factors as well when drugs from different pharmacological classes are available to treat the same disorder.

| Factor 1 | Non-Psychotropic Therapeutic Effects

When there is more than one type of drug to treat a specific disorder (e.g., lithium vs. valproate (Depakene, Depakote) for the treatment of bipolar disorder), drug selection is based, in part, upon on the presence of a co-existing medical condition such as a seizure disorder. This might mandate, for example, the use of an anticonvulsant with psychotropic properties such as valproate or carbamazepine for the treatment of bipolar disorder in a client with seizures (Sovner, 1991)

| Factor 2 | Side-Effects Profile

A consideration of the potential negative effects of psychotropic agents, especially those which may adversely affect the habilitative process (e.g., tricyclic antidepressants can impair short term memory), may be the deciding factor in drug selection. Constipating drugs (e.g., those with anticholinergic properties) would be avoided in clients with poor intestinal muscle tone.

| Factor 3 | Drug-Medical Illness Interactions

The effects of a drug on the client's preexisting medical illnesses, especially seizure disorders, are often important in determining drug selection. For example, tricyclic agents might be avoided in a depressed client with history of seizures, who has been seizure-free for several years and is no longer taking anticonvulsant therapy. They would be avoided because tricyclic agents can lower the convulsive threshold and might, therefore, precipitate a seizure.

| Factor 4 | **Drug-Drug Interactions**

The impact of a new drug on the metabolism of those drugs the client is already taking also should be considered in the drug selection process. Fluoxetine (Prozac), for example, can increase plasma carbamazepine levels and cause toxicity. Therefore, sertraline (Zoloft), another selective serotonin reuptake inhibitor, might be prescribed instead.

Summary

For a client to be considered to be a candidate for the pharmacotherapy of SIBs, the clinical team must be able to identify a drug-responsive emotional state or psychiatric disorder that contributes to the occurrence and maintenance of the targeted behavior. The choice of specific medications is based upon disorder characteristics, not the behavior, per se. A therapeutic trial should be conducted in the same way as a behavioral intervention, viz., there should be a diagnostic hypothesis, a specified outcome, and an objective treatment monitoring system.

EIGHT

Clinical Applications:
Psychosocial

Introduction

This chapter provides illustrations of the range of psychosocial interventions for self-injury used successfully with persons with developmental disabilities. Each views self-injury as a learned behavior that can be modified. As will become evident, the majority of the more recent illustrations based selection of intervention on information derived from functional diagnostics. Others, especially those using punishment procedures as the major intervention, demonstrated reduction in the SIBs in the absence of hypotheses about instigating or maintaining conditions. The latter illustrations, although differing from the functional diagnostic model articulated in this Manual, are presented to provide the clinician with knowledge of the full array of interventions reported to be successful in reducing SIBs in persons with developmental disabilities.

Consistent with the individualized diagnostic and program prescriptive emphasis of the Multimodal Functional Approach, selection of any one or a combination of these and similar procedures should be based on the functional hypotheses deemed most meaningful for each person. As described, SIBs may become functional and may be maintained by the effects of both positive reinforcement (i.e., reinforcement-motivated SIBs, sensory reinforcement) and negative reinforcement (i.e., escape- or avoidance-motivated SIBs). In some instances, multiple influences may be present. When the type(s) and source(s) of these maintaining reinforcement conditions can be identified, psychosocial interventions that remove, reduce, modify, or replace these sources of reinforcement can be effective in reducing or eliminating the SIBs. In summary, as SIBs typically occur in multiple and complex physical and social settings, and may reflect the influences of multiple biopsychosocial factors, successful psychosocial intervention programs for most persons will consist of a combination of approaches described in this chapter.

As the level of health risk associated with self-injury varies from client to client, selection of intervention approaches will be influenced somewhat by the severity and specificity of the self-injury and related collateral behaviors. Suppressive procedures may be selected to inhibit health-threatening self-injury when combined with positive procedures to insure development and maintenance of alternative skills of (a) gaining valued sensory and social stimulation and (b) coping with various aversive conditions.

Reinforcement-Motivated SIBs

In those instances in which the SIBs are presumed to be motivated by deprivation of valued reinforcing conditions (e.g., sensory stimulation, social attention), and thus maintained by their functionality in producing these reinforcers, interventions may include one or more of the following.

- **Alter antecedent stimulus events** that occasion SIBs and insure availability of the valued reinforcing events following behaviors other than SIBs. In this approach, the conditions that are discriminative for self-injury are modified or replaced by conditions that mark the occasion for alternative adaptive responding. Systematic reinforcement of the resulting alternative behaviors may be provided to insure maintenance of these new functional behaviors.

- **Teach functionally equivalent behavioral**

alternatives to SIBs as means of gaining access to the maintaining events or their equivalents. In functional equivalence training, an initial assessment is completed to identify the stimuli that instigate and those that maintain the self-injurious behaviors. Assessment information is used to devise a training program to teach a functionally equivalent and socially appropriate replacement for the aberrant behavior. Once acquired, this new skill will be controlled by the same instigating stimuli and consequences that previously controlled the aberrant responses. These functional alternatives may consist of motor responses that result in equivalent reinforcing events or may involve functionally equivalent communicative behaviors of a nonverbal or verbal nature.

- **Teach competing behaviors.** In those instances in which an appropriate behavior becomes self-injurious due to its excessive occurrence, the person may be taught an alternative incompatible behavior.

- **Follow an extinction procedure** of removing or minimizing the availability of reinforcing events following SIBs. Following implementation of this approach, the SIBs become nonfunctional as the previously contingent reinforcing consequences are eliminated.

- **Provide the maintaining reinforcing conditions on a noncontingent basis.** In this procedure, initial assessment is completed to identify the stimulus consequences that serve to maintain the self-injury. These reinforcing conditions are delivered on a time-based schedule independent of occurrence of the SIBs.

Alter Antecedent Stimulus Events

Intervention Tactic 1

Provide Enriched Stimulus Conditions

Favell et al. (1982) observed that the eye-poking, hand-mouthing and pica SIBs of young adults with profound mental retardation occurred primarily when socially isolated and unoccupied. An intervention program, based on the assumption that the SIBs were maintained by the resulting visual or gustatory sensory reinforcement, altered the antecedent stimulus conditions by providing toys which set the occasion for an appropriate alternative to SIBs. Under these enriched conditions, the adults had an opportunity to engage in toy play that provided sensory reinforcement similar to that associated with SIBs. Following demonstration of the value of this environmental alteration in producing substantial reduction of SIBs, an added component of external reinforcement of more appropriate conventional toy play resulted in further reduction. In each case, the self-stimulation produced by the toys involved the same sensory modality as that associated with SIBs, i.e., clients who eye-poked used the toys to produce visual self-stimulation, those who engaged in hand-mouthing and pica began chewing the toys. These results emphasized the value of matching the sensory activities provided by the intervention program with the sensory stimulation involved in the self-injury.

Smith et al. (1993) used a pretreatment functional analysis to identify sensory (automatic) reinforcement as the maintaining condition for SIBs presented by a 40-year-old-woman who frequently used a wheelchair due to an unsteady gait and frequent falls. SIBs involved head slapping and punching and head banging against hard objects that resulted in contusions, swelling, and occasional lacerations. Treatment consisted of providing an enriched environment involving access to increased visual stimulation and a greater variety of stimulus materials with which to interact. Self-injury rapidly decreased to infrequent occurrence under these enriched sensory stimulation conditions.

Intervention Tactic 2

Provide Alternative Stimulation via Gross Motor Activities

Lancioni et al. (1984) and Baumeister and MacLean (1984) used a similar program approach of providing alternatives to SIBs as means of gaining sensory stimulation. Lancioni et al. (1984) were successful in reducing the self-injurious tantrums of three adolescents with multiple handicaps by providing daily periods of gross motor activities designed to provide a variety of sensory input. These periods lasted about 15-20 minutes each and totalled from 1 to 3 hours daily. The tantrums occurred infrequently but were severe and appeared unrelated to specific environmental events. The gross motor activities were selected as the therapeutic approach based on the assumption that the self-injurious tantrums were being maintained by the sensory consequences produced. By providing a more acceptable means of obtaining sensory stimulation through various gross motor activities, the tantrums apparently became less functional and reduced in frequency and duration.

Reductions of SIBs and stereotypic responding also were reported by Baumeister and MacLean (1984) with two young adult males with severe mental retardation. Neither had responded significantly to previously provided behavior modification programs involving a range of reinforcement and punishment procedures nor to various drug therapies. Both were provided an exercise program consisting of a daily one-hour jog. The distance covered increased from one mile per hour during the first week to three miles per hour during a six-week period. Self-injurious responding and stereotyped movements systematically decreased over the course of the exercise program. These therapeutic effects were lost upon termination of the exercise program, however, suggesting a need for a long-term and routine exercise program that would provide routine sensory and social stimulation.

Teach Functionally Equivalent Alternative Behaviors

Intervention Tactic 3

Functionally Equivalent Motor Responses

Steege et al. (1989) reported a significant reduction in the chronic self-injurious mouthing and biting of a severely multiply handicapped 8-year-old boy (Ron) who attended a public school program. Functional diagnostics indicated that Ron engaged in high-rate self-injury when in solitary conditions (toileting and positioning), resulting in the hypothesis that the SIBs served a self-stimulatory function. The SIBs were replaced by an alternate response of pushing a microswitch which activated either a fan or a radio, both stimulus conditions that previously had been demonstrated to be reinforcing to Ron. This alternative functional motor response of producing sensory stimulation remained dominant over the SIBs at 6-month follow-up.

Intervention Tactic 4

Functionally Equivalent Communication Skills: Overview

In persons with severely and profoundly impaired cognitive features, limited communication skills, and few alternative social behaviors, aberrant responding may represent effective and efficient means of insuring social feedback or of communicating about one's needs. A number of writers, in fact, suggest that such severe behavior problems as aggression, self-injury, and agitated/disruptive episodes may serve the same functions as other socially acceptable forms of verbal and nonverbal communication (e.g., Carr & Durand, 1985; Durand, 1990). The socially appropriate forms of communication either are not in the person's repertoire or else are relatively ineffective or inefficient means of communication. The aberrant behaviors in these instances may represent means of communicating wishes, concerns, or physical/psychological states such as pain or dysphoria. This COMMUNICA-TION HYPOTHESIS, using communication as a metaphor, suggests the program strategy of replacing the aberrant behaviors with alternative functionally equivalent forms of communicative skills of obtaining individually relevant positive consequences or of reducing, terminating, or avoiding conditions that are aversive to specific persons. For the individual with minimal functional social or expressive language skills, this would involve teaching the person specific other means of expressing his or her needs or wishes through the use of verbal or nonverbal communication skills.

To emphasize, this communication hypothesis of aberrant behaviors results in an educative skill development focus of intervention. Thus, functional communication training involves the teaching of alternative and functionally equivalent communicative responses as replacements for problem behavior (Bird et al., 1989; Durand, 1990; Durand & Kishi, 1987). Functional communication training differs from other differential reinforcement procedures. Of significance, the schedule of reinforcement is controlled by the participant. Carr and Durand (1985) and Wacker et al. (1990) suggest that this control feature of functional communication training reflecting the active participation of the client represents a primary variable in its success. Although these procedures involve reinforcement of behaviors other than the SIBs (as in DRO, DRI, DRA), the nature of the behavior selected as the target for reinforcement has specific qualities.

In identifying the alternative responses to be reinforced in functional communication training, behaviors are selected that are functionally equivalent to the SIBs, that is, ones that will produce the same results for the person. This selection requires functional diagnostics to identify the specific function or functions served by the SIBs. Once this function is identified (or presumed), any behavior, **verbal** or **nonverbal**, that produces the same effect may be selected as the teaching target. Critical in this analysis is identification of the specific positive or negative reinforcers that are produced by the SIBs, that is, those that represent the maintaining conditions, e.g., preferred activities, attention, assistance, time away from an activity, tangibles, and the like. Initially, for an alternative functionally equivalent behavior to be learned, the type of reinforcers provided must be specific to the person's communicative request. In addition, the requested reinforcers must be delivered on a schedule determined by the person's newly acquired communication requests. Reinforcement occurs on a continuous reinforcement schedule with a minimum of delay between the communicative behavior and reinforcement. As noted by Bird et al. (1989) "as a result, at the specific time when a specific environmental change is desired by the subject, a specific communicative response is available that can change the environment as consistently as his maladaptive behavior had in the past" (p. 46). Under these conditions, the alternative communicative response gradually becomes as effective and efficient, and as habitual or automatic, as the previously exhibited SIBs.

Experience with functional communication training has demonstrated convincingly that functional equivalents for SIBs become the most dominant behavior only after the person begins to demonstrate spontaneous use of these replacement behaviors in the natural setting rather than relying on prompts from others. This observation emphasizes that, even though alternative means of communicating concerns are in the person's repertoire, these are unlikely to become predominate over the SIBs until the person has experienced consistent success in the spontaneous use of these behaviors. Shifting the control of the reinforcing events to the person's alternative behavior and insuring, at least initially, that it is as effective and efficient in gaining access to these events appear to be critical components in the success of functional communication training (Bird et al. 1989; Carr, 1988; Horner & Day, 1991).

Merely teaching new communicative skills does not insure that a person will begin to use their newly-acquired behaviors as functional alternatives to chronically occurring aberrant behaviors. This was illustrated by Duker et al. (1991) in a training effort to decrease self-injurious and other disruptive behaviors in a group of children and adults (14 subjects ranging in age from 11 to 35 years) with severe and profound mental retardation. The authors assumed that the aberrant behaviors were serving a communicative function and therefore taught the clients a number of gestures (signs) which would enhance their ability to communicate wants and needs to caretakers. While self-injury and destructive behaviors showed decreases following training, other inappropriate behaviors (i.e., aggression, screaming, stereotypic behaviors, throwing objects, tearing clothes, and pica) were not significantly affected. These results would support the need to determine the specific functionality of each aberrant behavior as a basis for selecting behavior-specific interventions to address the specific instigating and maintaining conditions. Simply teaching communicative behaviors in an attempt to reduce aberrant behaviors in the absence of a thorough functional analysis is unlikely to yield consistent results among persons who present chronic behavior difficulties.

Other studies emphasize the need to teach functionally equivalent communicative behaviors under the stimulus conditions in which aberrant behaviors occurs. This was illustrated by Horner and Budd (1985) who taught an 11-year-old boy who was nonverbal and diagnosed as "autistic" to communicate wants and needs with manual signs. Systematic observation of antecedents and consequent events associated with aberrant behaviors indicated that these occurred under five different stimulus conditions such as presentation of food at lunch or beginning of language session.

Initially the boy, under conditions designed to simulate those under which the aberrant behaviors occurred, was taught an American Sign Language manual sign appropriate to each of five sets of stimulus conditions. Although sign learning occurred in this simulated setting, there was no generalization to natural settings in which the aberrant behaviors continued to occur. Following training of these communicative behaviors in the natural settings, however, the inappropriate behavior dropped to a near-zero level. The authors concluded that the communicative behavior "was brought under control of the same stimuli (in Natural Setting Training) as the inappropriate behavior, and resulted in the same consequences (i.e., teacher attention, access to target object) as the inappropriate behavior" (p. 44). These data support the previously stated conclusions that training programs must lodge communicative behaviors in the specific context (instigating and maintaining) under which the aberrant behaviors have gained functionality. This practice is illustrated in the forthcoming sections on teaching functionally equivalent communication skills.

The reader should consult Durand (1990) and Reichie and Wacker (1993) for a thorough presentation of the rationale, procedures, and case applications of functional communication training.

Intervention Tactic 5

Functionally Equivalent Nonverbal Communication Skills

Durand and Kishi (1987) taught young adults with severe/ profound mental retardation and dual sensory impairments either to sign or to present a token as a means of communicating their requests for staff attention or access to favorite objects. Alternative forms of communication were selected as each had previously been unsuccessful in verbal language training. Functional diagnostics had produced the hypothesis that SIBs were serving these communicative functions prior to training. Following training, significant reductions in SIBs were observed in those instances in which staff consistently responded to the communicative requests.

Intervention Tactic 6

Functionally Equivalent Verbal Communication Skills

Carr and Durand (1985) demonstrated through functional diagnostics that, when provided task demands in an educational setting, a group of four children with developmental disabilities frequently engaged in various disruptive behaviors including self-injury. It was hypothesized that the disruptive behaviors of two of the children were serving as nonverbal means of communication that had become functional in obtaining teacher attention. These children were taught a verbal communication response "Am I doing good work?" to solicit the teacher attention that previously had followed the disruptive behaviors. This communicative inquiry resulted in prompt teacher response consisting of variations of the sentence, "I like the way you're working today. You're putting all the pictures where they belong!" Verbal praise was accompanied by smiles and nods as well as physical approval such as tickling and pats on the back. The self-injury and other disruptive behaviors reduced to infrequent occurrence as the newly acquired verbal communication skills replaced the function served previously by the problem behaviors.

In an additional demonstration of teaching a functionally equivalent communicative behavior to replace SIBs maintained by positive reinforcement, Day et al. (1988) utilized functional communication training to decrease self-biting in a 9-year-old boy with moderate mental retardation and autism. Functional assessment revealed that the SIBs were reinforcement motivated in that high rates were observed under positive reinforcement conditions (SIBs resulted in access to edibles, objects or activities which previously had been offered to subject's peers in a group situation), and particularly following removal of the reinforcer. Training verbal responses to the phrase "Tell me what you want", following removal of a reinforcer (**reinforcer request training**) and to request alternative reinforcers when the initial request was denied (**denial training**), resulted in significantly lower rates of SIBs which were sustained over the 5-month intervention. Additionally, the duration of self-injurious episodes decreased from baseline levels of up to 30 minutes to single brief responses in most instances following training.

| Intervention Tactic 7 |

Teach Competing Behaviors

McNally et al. (1988) successfully reduced polydipsia in a young woman (Ms. P.) with severe mental retardation who presented a history of multiple hospitalizations for emergency medical treatment for water intoxication. While residing in a treatment unit of a residential facility, access to liquids was available only through requesting drinks from staff. At the end of each 30-minute interval throughout the day, staff presented Ms. P. with a choice of either consuming or refusing a 4-ounce glass of liquid (water or orange juice). The reinforcement qualities of choosing the liquid was diminished by (a) increasing the difficulty of drinking it by requiring that it be consumed through a narrow straw and (b) following this choice by a low-preference required activity (e.g., vocational work activity tasks). In contrast, water refusal was reinforced with edible rewards and by a period of no required activity. Finally, the salience of the options was emphasized by visually displaying the edible and merely asking Ms. P. if she wanted water. As success was obtained, the time intervals were increased to 45 minutes and finally to 60 minutes. This program of providing differential consequences for water consumption versus water refusal served to stabilize water intake. Additionally, there was a decrease in periods of agitation associated with attempts to obtain water at times other than the scheduled period.

| Intervention Tactic 8 |

Extinction of Reinforcement-Motivated SIBs

In following an extinction procedure, the consequences such as social attention or access to materials or activities presumed to strengthen and maintain SIBs are no longer provided on a contingent basis. In most instances, self injury as a learned behavior develops over an extended period of time through a process of differential reinforcement. As reinforcement typically does not follow every instance of self-injury, SIBs of high rate and major severity may be produced and maintained by a schedule of infrequent reinforcement. As a result, the self-injury becomes highly resistant to extinction. Additionally, during extinction the SIBs may increase in rate and intensity to a level that cannot be ignored. In view of these features, extinction as an intervention procedure seldom is used in isolation.

Self-injurious behaviors presumed to be strengthened and maintained by the resulting **sensory stimulation**, however, differ from those resulting from environmental consequences. The sensory consequences are on a continuous schedule of reinforcement rather than intermittent as each self-injurious behavior produces sensory consequences. As a result, extinction is likely to occur more rapidly and becomes a viable treatment approach for SIBs maintained by sensory consequences. This extinction process of sensory-maintained SIBs is illustrated by Rincover and Devany (1982) and Blankenship and Lamberts (1989). In these demonstrations, the therapists used a procedure of masking the sensory consequences of the self-injury.

Rincover and Devany (1982), in treatment of young children with profound mental retardation whose self-injury appeared to be self-stimulatory and thus presumed to be maintained by the sensory stimulation produced, demonstrated the value of a sensory extinction procedure in immediately and substantially reducing SIBs. In using this procedure, the sensory stimulation associated with the specific SIBs of each child was removed. In illustration, one boy who engaged in head banging was provided a helmet which attenuated the tactile sensory consequences of the SIB. Another child, who engaged in self-injurious face scratching, was required to wear thin rubber gloves. This procedure prevented the child from damaging her skin but, although significantly reducing the sensory stimulation, did not prevent her from scratching.

Blankenship and Lamberts (1989) provide further support for the utility of removing the sensory stimulation involved in SIBs. These therapists reported a rapid and significant reduction in self-injurious cheek gouging and face slapping in two women with profound mental retardation through contingent application of a five-minute duration of wearing a helmet with an opaque face screen. Results were maintained at low levels over a 6-month maintenance period. These treatment effects were viewed as supporting the hypothesis that the SIBs were being maintained by the reinforcing properties of the heightened sensory input resulting from the SIBs. Following reduction of the sensory input, the self-injurious cheek gouging and face slapping decreased.

> Intervention Tactic 9

Provide Noncontingent Reinforcement

Vollmer et al. (1993) demonstrated the value of noncontingent reinforcement (NCR) in reducing the chronic and severe self-injurious behaviors of three female adults diagnosed as demonstrating either severe or profound mental retardation. A functional analysis identified social attention as a potential source of positive reinforcement maintaining the SIBs. These adults were provided two treatment conditions: NCR and DRO. The DRO intervention provided social reinforcement following periods of time during which SIBs were absent. If SIBs occurred at any time during the interval, the time was started again. During the NCR period, social attention was provided on a fixed-time schedule in which the person's behavior did not influence the frequency of reinforcement. Results showed that both procedures were highly effective in reducing self-injury, probably because the functional reinforcer (social attention) for self-injury was used during treatment. The NCR condition would be preferred in view of its ease of delivery.

Escape-Motivated SIBs

For those self-injurious behaviors assumed to be escape-motivated and thus functional as they remove, reduce, or postpone aversive conditions, a number of management and treatment interventions may be useful. These involve approaches designed to accomplish the following.

- **Remove the aversive antecedent conditions.** In this approach, the SIBs are managed by removal of the instigating stimulus conditions.

- **Reduce the aversive qualities of antecedent conditions.** In this approach, the motivation for the SIBs is decreased.

- **Remove the maintaining contigency through extinction.** The SIBs become nonfunctional as these do not result in escape from or avoidance of the aversive stimulus events.

- **Use compliance training** (this procedure includes an escape-extinction component). In
  instances in which SIBs are used to escape
  from aversive task demands, compliance training insures that this source of reinforcement is
  no longer forthcoming.

- **Teach functionally-equivalent behaviors**.
  In this approach, behaviors are taught that
  serve the same function as that associated
  with SIBs.

> Intervention Tactic 10

Remove the Aversive Antecedent Conditions

Although escape-motivated SIBs may be managed by removal
of the aversive stimulus conditions that instigate these behaviors, the
procedure does not reduce the likelihood of recurrence of SIBs if the
person is again confronted with these stimuli. Touchette et al. (1985)
provide illustration of this behavior management procedure and its
potential value and limitations. Conducting an initial analysis of the
times and situations in which the SIBs of a young adult occurred, it was
discovered that the self-abuse was evident principally during the late
afternoon and evening hours. Increased self-hitting correlated with the
staff person assigned, the afternoon activities, and the number of peers
present. In an attempt to alter the controlling antecedents, the a.m. staff
was assigned to the late afternoon and the afternoon staff worked during
the morning. All other correlated events remained the same. With this
change in staff, the SIBs now occurred predominately in the morning. A
reversal of staff assignments correlated with a total reversal of the times
during which the self-abuse occurred. In this instance, the therapists
were able to manage the SIBs by identifying and removing the specific
staff that were highly correlated with the occurrence of the SIBs. As
noted, however, this management approach is incomplete as an inter-

vention approach as it leaves the person vulnerable on future exposure to the controlling effects of the stimulus conditions. Additional approaches designed to reduce or remove the aversive components of these antecedent conditions or to teach the person functional alternatives when confronted with these events would be necessary.

| Intervention Tactic 11 |

Reduce the Aversive Qualities of Antecedent Conditions

In this approach, an attempt is made to change the aversiveness of the avoidance-producing stimuli. If SIBs are functional in terminating teacher or task demands, in illustration, aspects of the stimulus complex that are aversive are identified and altered. As the aversive qualities of the stimulus complex are reduced, the motivation for the SIBs decreases.

Weeks and Gaylord-Ross (1981) and Carr et al. (1976) demonstrated the value in reducing SIBs of altering the escape-producing antecedent stimuli as a means of reducing or eliminating the aversive and discriminative properties of these antecedents. Weeks and Gaylord-Ross (1981) demonstrated initially that the self-injurious hand and finger biting behaviors of a 13-year-old girl with a diagnosis of severe mental retardation and autism varied as a function of the difficulty level of instructional tasks presented in a day school program. Virtually no SIBs occurred in easy tasks, but self-injury increased significantly as the number of errors increased when presented with difficult tasks. The difficult task presentation was changed to an errorless learning procedure using a stimulus fading sequence. As with the easy task, low rates of both errors and SIBs were observed under this revised teaching condition. The SIBs thus were managed by altering the aversive components (difficulty level) of the tasks.

As a second illustration of this approach, Carr et al. (1976) initially demonstrated that an 8-year-old boy with a dual diagnosis of "schizophrenia" and mild mental retardation consistently engaged in a high rate of self-injurious head and face slapping and hitting when presented with various verbal directives requiring motor responses. During free time and when presented verbal statements that did not require a response, near-zero rates of SIBs were evident. Under the hypothesis that the SIBs were escape-motivated, these therapists embedded the demands in the context of positive ongoing interactions. Under this condition, the therapist would relate a simple story in an animated, cheerful and entertaining manner and then present a directive within this positive context. The SIBs immediately dropped to a low level.

In alternating the verbal directives alone with a condition in which these demands were presented within the positive context, there was always an abrupt decrease in the rate of hitting in the positive context and an equally abrupt increase in the verbal directives alone condition. The therapists thus demonstrated that the SIBs could be managed by altering the aversiveness of the directives. Apparently the positive context produced emotional responses that served as setting conditions for compliance behaviors. In support of this thesis, the therapists described the child as smiling and laughing and appearing to be quite happy. On removal of this setting event, however, presentation of a directive resulted in SIBs. There had been no lasting reduction in the aversive qualities of the verbal directives.

Although not demonstrated, it could be expected that through continued association with a positive context, the directives would gradually lose their aversive qualities. If accomplished, instruction-following behaviors would continue to occur as the positive context was faded. The addition of consistent positive reinforcement following compliance in this context should also contribute to reducing the aversive qualities of the directive.

Extinction of Escape-Motivated SIBs

In using an extinction procedure, the aversive antecedent stimulus conditions are continued and the person is not permitted to escape or avoid these following SIBs. In illustration, if SIBs occur following the presentation of a work task requirement, the directive to complete the task would continue until the task is completed. SIBs would be ignored or blocked. An extinction procedure used in isolation would not be the treatment of choice in persons with severe SIBs and/ or with limited behavioral repertoires due to the typical gradual reduction in SIBs and to the observation that reduction may be preceded by an increase in rate of occurrence. These potential difficulties are consistent with the pattern of "getting worse before getting better" often associated with the extinction of behaviors maintained by positive reinforcement. In most instances, a procedure of guided compliance training, which contains an escape-extinction component, would be combined with differential reinforcement of compliance behavior.

Intervention Tactic 12

Extinction, Compliance Training, and Differential Reinforcement Procedures

As suggested, the extinction procedure typically is used within a guided compliance training program. In this approach, the person is guided to engage in the behaviors required by the demand condition. In illustration, if SIBs occur following an instructional directive, the person would be physically guided to engage in the behaviors requested, with the SIBs either ignored or blocked. Full physical guidance would be faded into physical prompts as permitted by progress. Physical prompts would next be replaced by a firm verbal directive and faded further into the typical verbal directive. Reinforcement would be provided for task completion. High preference reinforcers provided during initial training for compliance would have two beneficial effects. First, the strength of instruction-following would increase. Secondly, the aversiveness of the tasks would be reduced through pairing with receipt of the preferred reinforcer.

As an illustration of extinction through use of a compliance training procedure, Iwata et al. (1990) initially selected children whose SIBs occurred frequently in conditions containing aversive events and were judged to be escape-motivated. In an instructional setting, various task demands were presented. Compliance was socially reinforced. If SIBs occurred, the child was physically guided through to task completion. Following implementation of extinction plus physical guidance, SIBs decreased to zero or near-zero and compliance increased noticeably. A maintenance and generalization program was implemented in each child's ongoing instructional programs and consisted of continued use of the extinction plus physical guidance procedure combined with reinforcement.

| Intervention Tactic 13 |

Extinction and Altering Antecedents

A number of writers have described variations of a procedure for treatment of noncompliance that involves presenting a set of directives for which there is a high likelihood of compliance immediately preceding a directive that is unlikely to be followed. This procedure has been described as task variation (Dunlap, 1984), embedding (Carr and Carlson, 1993), pretask requesting (Singer et al., 1987) and behavioral momentum (Mace et al., 1988). These writers have reported improvement in compliance following use of this procedure.

Zarcone et al. (1993a) combined this procedure with extinction in successfully reducing the SIBs (head banging against hard surfaces) of Ethel, a 33-year-old woman diagnosed as presenting profound mental retardation. A functional analysis indicated that the SIBs were maintained by excape from instructions. During treatment, instructions with a high probability of resulting in noncompliance and SIBs were immediately preceded by other instructions that typically resulted in compliance. In addition, SIBs were followed by escape-extinction, that is, Ethel was provided prompts and physical guidance to insure compliance and no escape. When presented alone, the high-probability sequence did not reduce self-injurious behaviors. In contrast, extinction used alone did produce a treatment effect. Maximum reduction, however, was obtained when the high-probability sequence was combined with escape extinction. The writers suggested that extinction may be a necessary component of treatment of SIBs maintained by escape.

In a companion study, escape-extinction was compared with an extinction condition that also included a fading component (Zarcone et al., 1993b). In this study involving three adult women with profound mental retardation, the frequency of instructions was initially reduced to zero and then was gradually faded back in until the instructional rate matched that of the original baseline. Extinction alone reduced SIBs in fewer session than did extinction plus fading. However, an extinction burst was observed at the onset of treatment with extinction that was not observed when combined with the fading component. As suggested earlier, the decision to use an extinction procedure in isolation is dependent upon the rate and severity of the SIBs during the extinction burst. The SIBs may increase beyond acceptable limits before these are reduced.

$$\boxed{\text{Intervention Tactic 14}}$$

Teach Functionally Equivalent Communication Skills: Nonverbal

Bird et al. (1989) used functional communication training to treat high levels of several SIBs exhibited by Greg, a 27-year-old male with diagnoses of autistic disorder and profound mental retardation. Greg's expressive language skills were limited to approximately 15 one-word utterances that were seldom spontaneous and often difficult to interpret. He required physical prompting to complete most of his activities of daily living routines while attending a day program. Greg's SIBs had resulted in detachment of both retinas, leaving him blind. At the initiation of functional communication training, he was provided one-on-one staffing due to the severity of his SIBs. A range of medical and behavioral interventions had been attempted with only minimal success. The most recent behavioral interventions in effect prior to initiating the functional communication skills training program consisted of differential reinforcement procedures (DRO, DRI) combined with response interruption, reprimand, and overcorrection.

Assessment of the possible functions served by Greg's SIBs

suggested an escape-from-task-demands hypothesis. The functional communication training program taught Greg an alternative nonverbal (exchanging a plastic token) but functionally equivalent means of escape, that is, obtaining a break from task demands presented in his classroom program. An immediate and substantial reduction in self-injurious episodes was obtained. These results were maintained with introduction of successive task demands of increasing difficulty and duration and also generalized across the three teachers who worked with Greg. Additionally, there was a concurrent increase in (a) Greg's spontaneous verbal requests to initiate work even during periods of time when he had an opportunity to avoid work demands completely, and (b) spontaneous verbal requests for food, a behavior that seldom occurred prior to the training program.

Intervention Tactic 15

Teach Functionally Equivalent Communication Skills: Verbal

Carr and Durand (1985) demonstrated the value of teaching an alternative verbal communication response in reducing escape-motivated SIBs. After it was initially demonstrated that children with developmental disabilities attending a day school program engaged in SIBs when presented difficult instructional tasks, these children were taught a verbal response as a means of soliciting teacher assistance. This training consisted of three stages. The child initially was prompted by the teacher to say "I don't understand." Following consistent correct imitation of this verbal behavior, the child was presented with a difficult task. When an error was made, the teacher said "That's not correct!" and added "Do you have any questions? Say "I don't understand." When correctly imitated, the teacher replied "O.K. I'll show you" and through use of gestures and verbal statements demonstrated the correct response. In the final training stage, the teacher's verbal prompts were faded until the child responded correctly to the inquiry "Do you have any questions?"

Following training, SIBs and other disruptive behaviors reduced to infrequent occurrence. Through learning an alternative verbal response that resulted in adult assistance on difficult tasks, the children experienced less failure. This reduction in aversiveness of the tasks reduced the motivation for the SIBs.

In a successful replication of these results demonstrating functionally equivalent skill development as replacements for aberrant behaviors maintained by negative reinforcement, Durand and Carr (1991) also assessed maintenance and transfer across teachers and classrooms over 18 to 24 month time periods. The challenging behaviors (SIBs, tantrums, screaming, physical aggression) of three boys attending a school program for children with developmental disabilities were assessed as being maintained by escape from academic demands. Each child was taught alternative functional communication responses that resulted in teacher assistance ("I don't understand" or "Help me"). Following training of these new communicative skills, a substantial reduction in challenging behaviors of each boy was noted. Further, these results transferred across new tasks, environments, and teachers. Finally, the results were generally maintained from 18 to 24 months following functional communication training. In one instance, brief booster sessions were used to reduce articulation difficulties of a child to insure that the functional communicative response was understandable to the teacher. The writers suggested that the maintenance and transfer of the intervention gains to new settings could be attributed to the introduction of natural maintaining conditions. The new communicative behaviors served to solicit the desired consequences even from teachers who were unaware of and untrained in the functional communication training procedures.

> Intervention Tactic 16

Combine Functional Communication Training with Extinction and Punishment

While recognizing that functional communication training (FCT) is a valuable treatment for SIBs, especially when a functional analysis has clearly implicated specific positive or negative reinforcement maintaining conditions, Fisher et al. (1993) noted that the sources of reinforcement may be unclear in a substantial number of cases involving self-injury. In these instances a multicomponent treatment package may be required to obtain maximum effects. In seeking the most effective treatment for clients with profound mental retardation and limited expressive language skills who had been hospitalized for treatment of destructive behaviors, these clinicians evaluated combinations of FCT, extinction, and punishment. The punishment procedure was client-specific and consisted either of a 30-second basket-hold time-out or a requirement to complete five requests (e.g., picking up materials thrown five times) following an episode of destructive behavior. With most of the clients, FCT was not sufficient to produce clinically significant reduction in destructive behaviors. When combined with punishment, generalized and enduring treatment effects were obtained. These results are consistent with those reported by Wacker et al. (1990) who suggested that both FCT and punishment may be necessary for maximum reductions in destructive behaviors. These clinicians also evaluated the relative effects of FCT, extinction, differential reinforcement of other behavior, and punishment as a means of selecting the most effective combination of intervention procedures.

In summary, in those clients who do not respond to FCT with a clinically acceptable reduction in their self-injurious and related destructive behaviors, it may be useful to add a mild punishment contingency to increase the person's motivation to select the alternative communicative response as a replacement for the SIBs.

Intervention Tactic 17

Multiply-Motivated Self-Injury

Often times, functional analysis of self injurious behaviors yields not one but several instigating and/or maintaining factors. Assessment may show, for instance, that although the SIBs occur at high rates under certain conditions (decreased staff attention) they may also occur during seemingly contrary conditions (staff interactions, requests, or demands). Functional diagnostics may indicate that the SIBs are reinforcement-motivated on some occasions and escape-motivated on other occasions. In such cases, addressing one factor through intervention typically leads to decreases in the problematic behavior. However, these decreases may not be sustained or sufficiently clinically significant until additional contributing factors are targeted.

Day et al. (1988) utilized functional diagnostics to discover multiple determinants of SIBs in several children with mental retardation. Functional assessment conditions employed included positive reinforcement, negative reinforcement, and sensory-input both alone and with a trainer present. In one case, Mary, a 15-year-old profoundly impaired adolescent with a history of SIBs since infancy, demonstrated high rates of SIBs under the positive reinforcement condition. Initial intervention consisted of teaching Mary to clap her hands in order to obtain trainer attention, and then to label or sign for desired items. Although this **request training** produced a significant decrease in SIBs, the effect was not sustained. Functional assessment of the behavior had also revealed a moderate level of responding during task demand situations. Therefore, **protest training**, in which Mary was taught to say "no" to terminate undesired tasks, was additionally implemented. Combination of the two procedures resulted in consistently low rates of SIBs.

Heidorn and Jensen (1984) successfully treated the severe and chronic SIBs of a 27-year-old male diagnosed as profoundly developmentally delayed. Due to the severity of the SIBs (rubbing his head on walls, floors, and other objects and digging his finger nails into his forehead and nose), the adult was placed in restraints almost 17 hours daily and provided various psychotropic medications. Previous SIBs of eye-poking had resulted in blindness in both eyes.

Functional diagnostics suggested that the self-injury was maintained by both positive and negative reinforcement. When left alone during free time, he would scream and engage in SIBs until someone talked to or touched him. Additionally, when placed in demand situations requiring his cooperation or compliance, SIBs would occur until the demand was removed. Although capable of dressing, feeding, and grooming himself independently, his SIBs had shaped the staff into completing these tasks for him.

Treatment during free time for the reinforcement-motivated SIBs involved extinction and differential reinforcement. Staff provided no verbal interaction, edibles, or physical contact immediately following self-injury but provided these following injury-free periods of variable duration.

In task demand situations in which escape-motivated SIBs occurred, graduated guidance was used to insure compliance. SIBs were prevented or redirected as the trainer guided the adult through to task completion. Upon completing the task, edibles, verbal praise, and physical contact were provided and the demand situation was terminated. If the client became agitated and attempted to hit or pinch the trainer, a relaxation procedure was implemented. On termination of agitation, he was returned to the task and prompted to completion. These procedures were implemented in various settings and with various tasks to enhance generalization and maintenance.

This multicomponent program consisting of (a) an extinction procedure plus a DRO for the SIBs assumed to be maintained by positive reinforcement and (b) a differential reinforcement for alternative behaviors (DRA) plus compliance training (containing an escape extinction component) for SIBs presumed to be escape-motivated resulted in significant reductions in self-injury. Subsequent reduction in medication coincided with an immediate increase in self-injury which gradually subsided. Additionally, on relocation to a new living unit within the facility and later to another facility serving persons with severe visual impairments, initial increases in SIBs occurred. These, again, decreased to near-zero levels as staff consistently implemented the program. Maintenance of these treatment effects were evident on frequent follow-up observations during the 35 months after placement. The man was participating fully in the unit routine, including being independent in self-feeding, and attending a regular school program.

Bird et al. (1989) provide a final illustration of the need to address multiple contributing conditions. Functional communication skills were taught to Jim, a 36-year-old male with profound mental retardation, who displayed severe aggressions and SIBs. Assessment had determined that Jim's behavior was escape-motivated (from demand situations) as well as reinforcement-motivated (desire for tangible rewards). Training, consisting initially of teaching Jim to sign for a break from task demands, resulted in immediate reductions in his aberrant behaviors. Jim was also trained in using signs to request reinforcers (music, food, bathroom, and work). As these alternative communicative behaviors became a functional part of Jim's behavioral repertoire, continued decreases in problem behaviors were seen. These low levels of 5 or less incidents per week compared to 25-75 incidents per week prior to training were maintained even when task demands, difficulty level, and task length were increased. Maintenance and transfer were also observed across changes in staff, programs, classroom site, and as the staff-to-client ratio decreased. A discrimination training component was added (red/green signs) to inform Jim of when his requests would be granted and when they would not. In addition to the decreases in aggression and SIBs, positive effects of training included an increase in Jim's on-task behavior and an overall increase in his spontaneous signing.

Intervention Tactic 18

Response Efficiency of Functionally Equivalent Behaviors

A range of studies demonstrating the usefulness of functional equivalence training have been described. As noted earlier, a critical factor suggested by a number of writers in the successful application of this training is that of response efficiency (Bird et al., 1989; Carr, 1988; Wacker et al., 1991). Horner and Day (1991) examined the role of the following three components of response efficiency relative to the acquisition and maintenance of functionally equivalent behaviors: (a) the **physical effort** required to perform the equivalent response, (b) the **schedule of reinforcement**, and (c) the **delay in time** between presentation of the discriminative stimulus for a target response and delivery of the reinforcer for that response.

A 12-year-old boy (Paul) with severe mental retardation and a six-year history of severe aggression (hitting, kicking, scratching) and self-injury (severe self-hits to his head) was used to evaluate the **physical effort** component. Functional assessment suggested that Paul's aberrant responding was maintained by escape from difficult tasks. He initially was taught the American Sign Language signs for "I want to go please." During presentation of training in self-care skills, use of the sentence resulted in an immediate 30-45 second break from task demands. During initial sessions, aggression decreased noticeably as Paul was using the functionally equivalent sentence to request a break. These gains were short-lived, however, as attempts to use the sentence declined and aggression showed a dramatic increase. Paul was next taught to sign "break" that required considerably less physical effort on his part. Under this condition, aggression decreased substantially and remained low. Additionally, even though Paul had an opportunity to escape the demand on each presentation of a task directive, he averaged 80% attempts to comply with directives during the training sessions. After learning the word sign, Paul made no further attempts to use the functionally equivalent sentence of "I want to go please."

The efficiency component of **schedule of reinforcement** was evaluated with a 14-year-old adolescent (Peter) with profound mental retardation and an 11-year history of severe self-injury. Functional assessment indicated that the aberrant behavior was functional in obtaining trainer assistance when he was provided difficult tasks. Initially, Peter was taught to sign "Help" as a functionally equivalent means of soliciting staff assistance. During a difficult picture-matching task, Peter was provided immediate staff assistance after he signed "Help" three times. Although an initial reduction in self-injury occurred, Peter's use of signing gradually decreased to near-zero and his self-injurious behavior returned to 95-100% of trials. After booster training to reestablish the "help" response, Peter was then provided assistance following each request. Under this reinforcement schedule, he signed for help on nearly every trial, attempted every trial, and engaged in no self-injurious behaviors. After reinstatement of the FR 3 schedule, a dramatic reduction in the use of the sign, a drop in Peter's attempts to complete the task, and an immediate increase in self-injurious behavior were noted. Return to the FR 1 schedule resulted in a drop in self-injury to near-zero as he again used the "help" sign on every trial and his attempts to complete the task returned to a near 100% level.

The final component of response efficiency, **delay of rein-forcement**, was demonstrated with Mary, a 27-year-old with a five-year history of severe self-injury and aggression. Assessment implicated escape-motivation as the maintaining condition. Initially, Mary was taught to hand the trainer a card with the word "BREAK" on it. A 1-second delay vs. a 20-second delay in providing a break from task demands were contrasted. Initially, a 20-second delay was imposed from the time Mary handed the card to the trainer until she was provided a break from task demands. Aggression increased under these conditions as Mary quickly discovered that she could escape from task demands faster through aggression. After a change to a 1-second delay, aggression reduced to low levels.

These results clearly suggest that newly taught equivalent behaviors will be used as replacements for aberrant responding in escaping from or in gaining assistance in dealing with aversive tasks only if these are as or more efficient in gaining reinforcement as is the aberrant responding. Most desirable results will be obtained when each of these three components of physical effort, schedule of reinforcement, and delay between the functionally equivalent response and the reinforcement are considered in designing a training program.

Additional Interventions

In addition to intervention programs designed to alter the conditions presumed to instigate and maintain SIBs, a number of approaches involving differential reinforcement, relaxation training, and punishment contingencies are available for use by the clinician. Use of these latter procedures, while not diagnostically established as related to the functionality of the SIBs, has been demonstrated in some instances to produce a reduction in the self-injury. However, while these nonspecific positive reinforcement, stimulus control, and behavior suppressive procedures may reduce self-injury, these effects are best maintained if correlated with interventions that do address the specific instigating and maintaining conditions.

```
Intervention Tactic 19
```

Teach Other Behavior Alternatives Through Differential Reinforcement

The procedure of differential reinforcement involves providing frequent and valued consequences for appropriate behaviors or for the nonoccurrence of the self-injurious acts during specific periods of time. The differential reinforcement procedure may consist of a DRO (reinforcement provided immediately following periods of time in which no self-injury occurs), a DRA (differential reinforcement of alternative behaviors that could physically occur at the same time as the SIBs), or a DRI (reinforcement provided for specific behavior that is both appropriate and physically incompatible with self-injury).

Lovaas et al. (1965) reduced the high-rate self-hitting behaviors of a 9-year-old boy to a near-zero level after systematically reinforcing him with smiles and praise for clapping his hands to music, an appropriate use of hands that replaced the SIBs. Weiher and Harman (1975), using a DRO procedure, reduced the chronic head banging of a 14-year-old boy with severe mental retardation to a near-zero level by providing applesauce at the end of various time intervals during which the SIBs did not occur. Regain and Anson (1976) used food reinforcers in a DRO procedure with a 12-year-old girl with severe mental retardation who, prior to intervention, spent much of her time engaging in self-scratching and head banging behaviors. Although not totally eliminated, these SIBs were significantly reduced under the DRO contingency.

Cowdery et al. (1990) used DRO to successfully treat severe and longstanding self-injurious behavior presented by a 9-year-old boy. Assessment revealed that the boy's scratching apparently was stereotypic and automatically reinforced. An escalating DRO schedule using token reinforcement (pennies) eliminated self-injurious behaviors for lengthy periods of time as reinforcement was provided throughout the day. Additionally, token reinforcement was demonstrated to be superior to DRO based on social reinforcement.

Tarpley and Schroeder (1979), in treatment of three adults with profound mental retardation, found a DRI procedure (i.e., providing ice cream or orange juice following periods of play activity and no SIBs) to be more useful than DRO (i.e., providing ice cream or orange juice following periods of no SIBs) in effectively reducing head banging.

As final illustration of reinforcement of alternatives incompatible with SIBs, Tierney (1986) taught a 14-year-old male with profound mental retardation to sit calmly in a chair on initiation of any SIBs.

Significant reduction in SIBs, consisting of slapping and punching his head and hitting his fingers and hands and often accompanied by screaming, jumping, running and/or clinging to the nearest person, coincided with reinforcement of an incompatible behavior of sitting calmly in a chair with hands resting on his knees. Twelve-month follow-up revealed maintenance of treatment gains.

```
Intervention Tactic 20
```

Use Differential Reinforcement and Self-Management

Grace et al. (1988) demonstrated the successful application of self-management and related reinforcement procedures in reducing the self-injurious behaviors of a 14-year-old adolescent (Tom) with a diagnosis of Lesch-Nyhan syndrome. The adolescent had lived at a large state residential facility since the age of five. He had a diagnosis of moderate mental retardation and was described as exhibiting severe impairments in verbal expression and motor control. During most of his 9 years of institutional living, Tom's legs and hands had been physically restrained due to his frequent and recurring biting of his hands and fingers. His front teeth had been removed in an attempt to limit his self-injury.

During treatment, the frequency of attempted and actual SIBs were obtained both (a) in a dayroom while Tom was spending periods of time unrestrained in his wheelchair with a group of peers positioned in front of a television set and (b) in a private bedroom. Tom initially was taught to self-assess occurrence or nonoccurrence of his hand-biting SIBs by nodding or pointing to a pictorial happy or sad face. During training, Tom was exposed to trainer modeling, guided practice, and performance feedback. On occasions of accurate self-assessment, he was provided with hugs; inaccurate self-assessment resulted in an immediate 30-second time out involving the trainer turning his back towards Tom.

During the second phase of training, a direct care staff member serving as the trainer, (a) set a large kitchen timer for 3-7 minute intervals, (b) prompted Tom not to engage in self-injury, and (c) left the room for the designated period of time. On return of the trainer, Tom was prompted to evaluate the occurrence or nonoccurrence of SIBs during the preceding time period. Verbal reprimands were used to consequate SIBs and verbal praise was provided for no self-biting. The time period between staff-prompted self-assessment was gradually increased to 1-hour intervals.

Prior to training, attempted and successful biting varied from 1 to 37 occurrences per half-hour sessions in the dayroom and from 1 to 60 in the bedroom area. Treatment, initially provided in the dayroom, produced an immediate reduction in SIBs; these were completely eliminated after three days of the self-management program. After treatment was expanded to include the bedroom, there was an immediate elimination of SIBs in that setting. SIBs in both settings were maintained at a zero-level during 19-week follow-up.

This demonstration is instructive in that all training was conducted by daily care staff. After training, the program required only the minimal time needed to prompt Tom to refrain from SIBs, set the timer, and then return at the designated period to consequate Tom's self-assessment. It also is significant in that it represents one of the less complex and more successful programs reported for persons with Lesch-Nyhan syndrome.

| Intervention Tactic 21 |

Use Differential Reinforcement and Physical Interruption

Differential reinforcement also has been used in combination with other procedures to treat SIBs. Azrin et al. (1982) and Azrin et al. (1988) reduced the severe and chronic self-injurious behaviors of adolescents and adults with severe and profound mental retardation to near-zero levels in both school and living settings. In using the DRI plus physical interruption procedure, reinforcement was provided following periods of no self-injury and occurrence of play, social, or other appropriate behaviors. This reinforcement procedure was combined with interrupting each self-injurious episode and requiring the person's hands to rest in his or her lap for 2 minutes. In the 1988 report, Azrin et al. demonstrated the superiority of this DRI plus interruption procedure over other procedures involving social extinction, DRO and DRI used alone, and interruption used alone. In addition, treatment effects were obtained in each person's living area following initiation of the DRI plus interruption procedure by the living area staff.

Intervention Tactic 22

Use Relaxation Training

In a novel approach to producing alternatives to SIBs, Schroeder et al. (1977) demonstrated that relaxation training of two adolescents with severe mental retardation and chronic high-rate head banging resulted in a physiological state that was incompatible with occurrence of the SIBs. Effects were short-lived, however, suggesting a more comprehensive intervention program for effective and durable results.

Steen and Zuriff (1977) used relaxation training with a 21-year-old woman with profound mental retardation. Full restraint had been used for three years prior to treatment to manage severe biting and scratching. High rates of SIBs occurred when restraints were removed.

Intervention consisted of training the woman to relax her hand and arm while providing her with a continuous schedule of food, praise, and physical contact. Restraints were gradually removed under these conditions. Training, requiring a total of 115 sessions, was successful in virtually eliminating the SIBs. Follow-up at one year revealed a continued low rate of self-injury.

Intervention Tactic 23

Use Punishment Procedures

Punishment procedures consisting of contingent removal of positive reinforcers or contingent presentation of aversive conditions may be useful in reducing SIBs, with no attempt made to alter the instigating or maintaining conditions. The elicited behaviors (increase in agitation, tantrum-like-behaviors, aggression) that may accompany the presentation of aversive conditions, however, may have deleterious effects on the overall treatment program.

The following represent descriptions of the range of procedures involving punishment contingencies. Due to the controversy over the use of operant punishment procedures as treatment for SIBs, the reader is encouraged to consult the National Institutes of Health Consensus Development Conference Statement on Treatment of Destructive Behaviors in Persons with Developmental Disabilities (1989), Repp & Singh (1990), and the recent critical review by Linscheid (1992).

Time-out From Positive Reinforcement

A time-out procedure, consisting of removing the person from the opportunity to obtain reinforcement immediately following each self-injurious episode, has been used successfully in reducing SIBs in some individuals. This procedure obviously would not be appropriate for those persons whose SIBs are related to boredom and need for increased social or sensory stimulation, or for SIBs that are reinforced negatively through removal of aversive conditions. Removing the person from the aversive environmental conditions following SIBs would increase rather than decrease the self-injury.

An underlying assumption in use of a time-out procedure is that the person, at the time of removal, is in an environment that is positively reinforcing. Contingent removal from this reinforcing environment would be aversive and would serve to suppress the SIBs. A report by Solnick et al. (1977) illustrates the need to insure, prior to selecting this treatment procedure, that reinforcing conditions are in fact present. The self-injury of an adolescent with severe cognitive impairment was not reduced significantly following initiation of a time-out contingency until the environment from which the person was removed was enriched through increased stimulating and reinforcing activities and objects. Following enrichment, the time-out was effective in suppressing the SIBs. In addition, the time-out procedure produces more favorable effects when used in combination with that of reinforcement of alternative behaviors.

Hamilton et al. (1967) demonstrated the effectiveness of a time-out in eliminating the head and back banging behaviors of adults with severe levels of mental retardation. Following treatment, the SIBs had not reoccurred at follow-up checks several months later. Similar results were reported by Wolf et al. (1964) who used time-out to eliminate the self-destructive behavior of a 3 1/2 year-old boy with mental retardation in both a hospital and home setting. Wolf et al. (1967) reported that 3 years later, the same child's SIBs were again eliminated using time-out, this time in a school setting. The SIBs were eliminated following a small number of time-out experiences in this setting, suggesting that the child's prior experience with the time-out contingency increased its effectiveness. Finally, in a study by Lucero et al. (1976), the self-injurious behaviors of three girls with profound mental retardation were markedly reduced by withdrawal of food on each occurrence of the behavior.

Movement Suppression Time-out

Matson and Keyes (1990) demonstrated the effectiveness of a version of time-out that involved directing the client to remain in a designated motionless position (movement suppression) for a specified period of time following self-injury. One adult with severe mental retardation who displayed a moderate rate of self-injury was required to stand still with his arms extended out to the sides. A second adult with a low rate of self-slapping was required to stand quietly in a corner with feet together, hands to sides, and face to the corner for one minute. Both had been unresponsive to previous treatments involving DRO and verbal reprimand. The addition of the movement-suppression time-out resulted in a rapid reduction to non-occurrence of the self-injury. Treatment effects were maintained over an 8-month follow-up period for one client.

Response Cost

Van Houton (1993) reported the successful use of soft hand weights (commonly used by joggers) in reducing SIBs assumed to be maintained by sensory reinforcement. Tom, a 10-year-old boy with a diagnosis of severe developmental disabilities engaged in SIBs consisting of hard face slaps that led to bruising, swelling, and hair loss. These SIBs occurred at high rate throughout the day, including mealtimes. Initially, hand weights were worn for a 10-minute daily period, and progressively increased to a 60-minute daily session. At the end of treatment, staff members were using the weights for 30 minutes twice a day following face slaps. The writer reported that this was done only occasionally for 3 weeks and was not required after that. Results of the study suggested that the hand weights may have reduced face slaps primarily through the increased response effort required.

Presentation of Aversive Consequences

A final set of procedures involving punishment consists of presenting an aversive or punishing event contingent on each occurrence of self-injury. When punishment effects are obtained, empirical studies report rapid and clinically significant results. However, as noted in the earlier discussion of punishment, if used in isolation or as the major intervention procedure, the therapeutic suppressive effects often will lessen. Additionally, due to the highly specific discriminations frequently made by the client, generalization across settings typically does not occur. For maximum therapeutic effectiveness, punishment procedures, when used, should thus be combined with those designed to teach and/or strengthen alternative behaviors that will produce readily available and naturally occurring reinforcers in the person's environments.

Overcorrection

Several reports have demonstrated the usefulness of overcorrection procedures in reducing SIBs. The most common form of overcorrection used with SIBs involves training in which the part of the client's body (e.g., head, arm) involved in the SIBs is moved to a series of positions where it is held for several seconds (Foxx & Bechtel, 1983). Harris and Romanczyk (1976) applied this type of overcorrection in treatment of chronic head and chin banging of an 8-year-old boy in both home and school settings. An immediate reduction in SIBs was obtained following implementation of overcorrection, initially in the school and later in the home. These results remained at near-zero levels in both settings at 9-month follow-up. Using a similar procedure of "forced arm exercise," deCatanzaro and Baldwin (1978) eliminated the head hitting behaviors of young boys with profound levels of mental retardation. The overcorrection procedure produced an initial reduction in SIB and was subsequently combined with a DRO procedure which reduced the SIBs to near-zero levels. The treatment effects were generalized by extending intervention to several different settings.

Overcorrection, used in combination with other procedures, has been favored by a number of therapists. Measel and Alfieri (1976) demonstrated the efficacy of a combination of DRI and overcorrection to eliminate the hand slapping and head banging behaviors exhibited by two boys with profound mental retardation. Johnson et al. (1982) successfully reduced a variety of SIBs in adults with profound retardation through overcorrection and differential reinforcement procedures. These therapists observed, however, that overcorrection alone produced most of the therapeutic effects. Azrin et al. (1975) combined three overcorrection approaches (autism reversal, required relaxation, and hand-awareness training) to significantly decrease the SIBs of 11 clients, 10 of whom exhibited severe or profound mental retardation. Analysis of benefits indicated that SIBs were reduced by 99%. However, the therapists speculated that this multicomponent approach would be most effective (1) with a client who possessed a high level of outward-directed behavior prior to intervention, or (2) if the social environment was one that strongly encouraged outward-directed activity.

Aversive Electrical Stimulation

Butterfield (1975) describes this technique as delivering a physically harmless but psychologically aversive electrical stimulus to the person's limb or back for a brief duration immediately following occurrence of self-injury. This procedure has been the topic of a number of research studies and has been reported as a generally effective method of initially suppressing self-injury. The only published exceptions to the effectiveness of shock are with persons presenting the

Lesch-Nyhan syndrome (Favell, 1982).

   Tate and Baroff (1966) virtually eliminated the high-rate SIB (head banging, self-hitting, self-kicking) of a severally visually impaired 9-year-old boy following implementation of a shock contingency. In addition, treatment was correlated with increased eating and decreased posturing, saliva-saving, and clinging behaviors. Similar results were obtained by Lovaas and Simmons (1969) with boys with severe levels of mental retardation. Desirable side effects following reduction of SIBs included reduced exploration of the environment. Merbaum (1973) described the use of electrical stimulation by a mother in treatment of the SIBs of her 12-year-old son. SIBs were reduced in both home and school settings. A 1-year follow-up indicated maintenance of the SIBs at a near-zero level, with the mother reporting that her son was "quieter, happier, and wonderful around the house."

   Linscheid et al. (1990) describe the effects on the longstanding, severe, and unmanageable self-injurious behaviors of five persons ranging in age from 11 to 22 years with severe to profound levels of mental retardation following treatment with a device called SIBIS (self-injurious behavior inhibiting system). A sensor module, worn on the client's head and concealed by a cap or hat, generates a radio signal following detection of blows to the person's face or head. This coded radio signal is sent to a stimulus module, generally worn on the client's leg, which delivers an electrical stimulus with a maximum intensity of 3.5 milliamps at 85 volts.

   Clients with whom SIBIS was used met the following criteria: (a) chronic SIBs involving forceful contact with the head that produced tissue damage (b) a history of treatment failure and (c) current uncontrolled SIBs requiring the use of protective equipment, restraint and/or drugs. In all five cases, contingent electrical stimulation delivered by SIBIS resulted in rapid and near-complete suppression of the severe SIBs. Controlled and anecdotal follow-up data on four of the clients suggested continued benefits and absence of detrimental side effects associated with use of the treatment.

Additional Procedures

Other procedures have been reported as effective in reducing self-injurious behavior. These include: **contingent physical restraint** (Rapoff et al., 1980); **contingent exercise** (Borreson, 1980; Luiselli 1984); **facial or visual screening** - the person's face is briefly covered with a terry cloth bib or some similar means of visual occlusion following the SIBs (Rojahn, & Marshburn, 1992; Watson et al., 1986); **water mist** - water mist is sprayed in the person's face following SIBs (Dorsey et al., 1980); **aromatic ammonia** - ammonia is held briefly under the person's nose following SIBs (Altman et al., 1978); **aversive tickling** - the person is tickled for a prolonged period following SIBs (Greene & Hoats, 1971); and a **rage reduction technique** - the person is physically restrained and forced to hit the therapist's hand (Saposnek & Watson, 1974).

Conditioned Avoidance

When punishment procedures are used, the therapist may pair "no" or a similar stimulus with the presentation of the aversive consequences. In this manner, "no" may acquire sufficient conditioned aversive properties to maintain suppression of the behavior when presented in the absence of the primary aversive event. This effect was illustrated by Lovaas and Simmons (1969) who, following the pairing of "no" with electrical stimulation, found that "no" presented in isolation served to maintain suppression.

Maintenance and Generalization of Treatment Effects

The primary objective of a psychosocial intervention program for SIBs is to obtain treatment effects that continue to be present under conditions and settings differing from those involved in treatment. If, following systematic training by a language therapist in a classroom setting, a child learns an effective functionally equivalent nonverbal communicative response as a replacement for SIBs under demand conditions, this new behavior would be expected to continue to occur in the future in the presence of other instructors and in other settings.

Although only minimal systematic research has specifically addressed the problem of generalization and maintenance following treatment of self-injury, some promising guidelines are evolving from recent studies based on the functional analytic model. These suggest that generalization and maintenance of treatment effects may be enhanced under the following conditions.

For SIBs maintained by positive reinforcement:

Intervention Tactic 24

1. Establish the functionality of the SIBs.

2. Eliminate the functionality through extinction.

3. Provide equivalent positive reinforcement for alternative prosocial behaviors. Insure that the reinforcement schedule and type is equal to or exceeds that previously associated with SIBs.

4. These program approaches were demonstrated in the previously described study by Heidorn and Jensen (1984).

Intervention Tactic 25

1. Establish the functionality of the SIBs.

2. Teach a functionally equivalent response as an effective and efficient alternative to the SIBs.

3. Provide reinforcement consistency to insure that this alternative behavior is as effective and efficient as the SIBs in gaining maintaining

reinforcers.

4. These program approaches were demonstrated in the previously described studies by Carr and Durand (1985), Durand and Kishi (1987), and Stegge et al. (1989).

For SIBs maintained by negative reinforcement:

Intervention Tactic 26

1. Establish the functionality of the SIBs.

2. Eliminate this functionality through extinction and compliance training.

3. Provide positive reinforcement for compliance and related replacement behaviors.

4. These program approaches were demonstrated in the previously described studies of Heidorn and Jensen (1984) and Iwata et al. (1990).

Intervention Tactic 27

1. Establish the functionality of the SIBs.

2. Teach a functionally equivalent response as an effective and efficient alternative to the SIBs.

3. Insure continued reinforcement of this replacement behavior by various persons in various settings.

4. This program approach was demonstrated in the previously described studies by Bird et al. (1989), Carr and Durand (1985), and Durand and Carr (1991).

Summary

SIBs may become functional and thus maintained by the effects of both positive reinforcement (i.e., reinforcement-motivated SIBs) and negative reinforcement (i.e., escape- or avoidance-motivated SIBs). When the type(s) and source(s) of the maintaining reinforcing conditions can be identified, psychosocial interventions that remove, modify, or replace these sources of reinforcement can be effective in reducing or eliminating the SIBs. A major focus of these interventions is that of teaching functionally-equivalent behaviors.

In the final chapter of this Treatment Manual, two case studies are described to illustrate the clinical process of (a) obtaining assessment information, (b) translating these data into diagnostic hypotheses relating to instigating and maintaining conditions, (c) selecting interventions based on these formulations, and (d) evaluating the utility of these interventions following implementation of the IIP.

NINE

CASE STUDIES

In this final chapter, two case studies are used to illustrate the development of a Multimodal Integrated Intervention Plan through use of diagnostic-intervention formulations. Attention is given to the translation of assessment data into a set of hypotheses about instigating and maintaining conditions. The process continues as each hypothesis is used to guide development of treatment and management interventions designed to modify these controlling influences.

CASE 1

Mr. Joel Stebbin, a 27-year-old man with profound mental retardation and no functional vision or speech, presents frequent episodes of self-injurious behaviors involving face slapping, head hitting, head banging against furniture and floor, and face and arm scratching. These SIBs, present for a number of years, have resulted in trials of a variety of psychotropic medications and physical and mechanical restraints including a helmet and arm splints. When not in a structured program, Mr. Stebbin isolates himself in his room. While typically responsive to social stimulation, he seldom initiates interactions with staff or peers. Although Mr. Stebbin previously had been

*provided numerous biomedical and psychosocial in-
tervention programs, none had been effective in
producing more than a temporary reduction in his
episodes of SIBs. A consultant was retained to guide
the staff through a comprehensive multimodal functional assessment and intervention program.*

Initial Data Collection

Staff from Mr. Stebbin's residential placement had completed
daily recordings for the previous three months of each episode of SIBs
throughout his waking hours. As illustrated in Table 9.1, information
had been recorded on a 3x5 inch card immediately after each episode.
Note that the data card included information relating to date/time of
occurrence, general context (location, activity/program), specific antecedents and consequences of each self-injurious episode as well as
other observations that may reflect potential setting stimulus conditions.

As depicted in Figure 9.1, staff recorded monthly total frequencies of self-injurious episodes of 74, 83, and 95 for this three month
period. As an initial step in the functional analysis, these data were
displayed as a.m. and p.m. frequencies (Figure 9.2) and further as the
number of a.m. and p.m. periods during each month in which SIBs did
not occur (Figure 9.3). This initial analysis was revealing in that, as
depicted in Figure 9.2, most episodes occurred after 12 noon. Further,
as depicted in Figure 9.3, episodes did not occur every afternoon. In
fact, although daily frequencies averaged from 2.47 to 3.17 episodes
over the three months, the SIBs were quite episodic, with some 2-3 day
periods of minimal occurrences followed by periods during which SIBs
occurred during both a.m. and p.m. periods and on consecutive days.
Although not depicted, the analysis revealed that episodes seldom
occurred on weekends. This analysis indicated that the complex of
factors producing the SIBs were not consistently present and, at this
point, appeared related to structured program activities provided during
the week.

Table 9.1 Completed Data Recording Card

NAME: *Joel S.*   **OBSERVER:** *D. Ford*   **DATE:** *3/14*

TIME: *2:15 pm*

CONTEXT:

Walking with group of peers to work activities program.

ANTECEDENTS:

John bumped into Joel and pushed him against the wall.

BEHAVIOR:

Immediately began face slapping and screaming.

CONSEQUENCES:

Held his arm. Reassured him that John was in front of him and would not bump him again. Calmed after 30-45 seconds.

OTHER OBSERVATIONS:

Insisted that I hold his arm until he arrived at his work station. Noticeably apprehensive and cautious in walking.

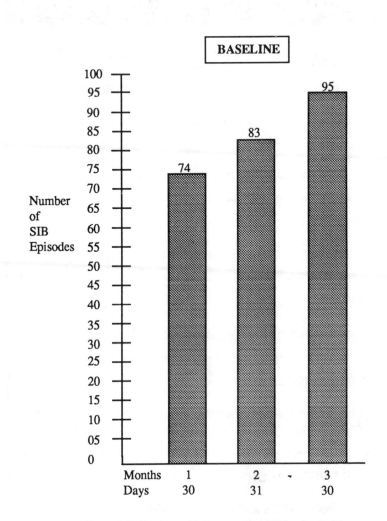

Figure 9.1. Total monthly frequencies of SIB episodes.

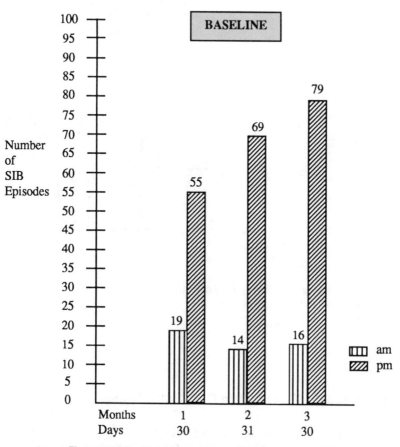

Figure 9.2. Total monthly frequencies of SIB episodes occurring during a.m. and p.m. periods.

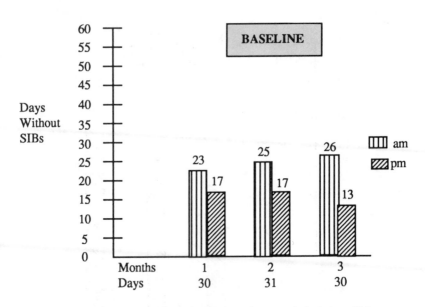

Figure 9.3. Monthly totals of a.m. and p.m. periods during which no episodes of SIBs occurred.

Medical and Psychiatric Considerations

Medical evaluation did not reveal any apparent primary or secondary medical contributors to the SIBs or to their increasing rates over the three month period. Additionally, there were no current or changing patterns of biological functioning that would be suggestive of possible psychiatric disorders, that is, no abnormalities were noted in eating, sleeping, irritability, or activity level other than the agitation associated with the SIBs. Although Joel tended to isolate himself when not in structured programs, he typically was responsive to staff requests to participate in both individual and small group activities. During these times, affective expression was positive. Staff did not report any change in social or affective responsiveness during the previous three month period except that noted during the SIBs episodes. On these occasions Joel displayed general emotional and motor agitation, with excessive body rocking, screaming and self-injurious acts of face and head slapping, head-banging, and face and arm scratching. As noted, however, on weekends these episodes were minimal. The only other cyclic nature of the episodes was between a.m. and p.m., with these time-of-day patterns disappearing on weekends when scheduled structured programming was minimal. Thus, neither medical nor psychiatric diagnostic formulations were offered as possible contributors to the SIBs or to account for the increases over the last three months.

Psychological and Socioenvironmental Considerations

In the absence of any apparent medical or psychiatric conditions or disorders as potential contributors to Joel's SIBs, the focus of the assessment shifted to a psychosocial functional analysis. As noted, a visual inspection of the frequency data displayed in Figure 9.2 revealed an obvious difference between a.m. and p.m. in number of self-injurious episodes, with most occurring in the afternoon. Further, episodes were unlikely on weekends. The initial focus of this functional analysis thus involved an examination of possible afternoon program experiences. This examination of Joel's program schedule indicated that the morning hours were spent in small group leisure or structured activities in small therapy rooms located adjacent to his living area. During these times, frequent staff contact was present and few program demands made. Afternoon hours, in contrast, were spent in structured programs involving large groups of peers, with greatly reduced individual staff contact. Additionally, in the afternoon, Joel was required to walk to and from various program locations some distance away from his living area.

To assist staff in gaining a view of the pattern of self-injurious responding and as a means of detecting potential conditions correlated with these episodes, the three-month data initially were evaluated relative to the general context of each episode. Data cards describing episodes that occurred in similar contexts were grouped together.

Grouping episodes with specific afternoon times/activities/locations was most informative. The **highest** number of self-injurious episodes occurred :

- during large group activities,
- in transition from one program location to another,
- in work activities that required continuous motor involvement, and

The **lowest** frequencies occurred:

- in small group programs during which frequent staff contact was provided, and
- on weekends during which minimal structured programming was offered.

In attempting to understand the increasing number of episodes across the three-month period, examination of his active treatment program schedule indicated that during the last week of Month 1, Mr. Stebbin had been assigned to a new program in the afternoon supervised by an unfamiliar staff. Additionally, during the first week of Month 3, he had been assigned to a large group program requiring mobility through a crowded area. Each of these program changes was followed by an increase in SIB episodes. Staff reported that Joel typically becomes noticeably agitated with any change in his routine, including being exposed to unfamiliar staff or settings/activities. Staff also offer the observation that it typically takes Joel a few weeks to adapt to changes.

A structured observation format was developed based on information obtained from the data cards and from staff narrative accounts of current episodes. With this format as an observational guide, additional data were obtained when Joel was exposed both to high and low risk conditions. Staff continued to complete data cards on each episode of agitation involving SIBs.

Diagnostic-Intervention Formulations

Based on the information obtained from the individual data

cards and follow-up direct observations, a series of hunches were developed about instigating and maintaining conditions. Each of these initial formulations was translated into related treatment and management intervention approaches. The Multimodal Functional Diagnostic Worksheet (see Figure 6.2) was used to guide the development of these diagnostic-intervention formulations. Staff next used the Diagnostic-Intervention Formulation Worksheet (Figure 6.3) to guide translation into the separate components of the Multimodal Integrated Intervention Plan (Figure 6.1).

Diagnostic Formulations: Instigating Conditions

In illustration of this process of identifying instigating conditions, the occurrence of self-injurious episodes occurring in large groups and in periods of time during transition and typically immediately preceding and following attendance at large group activities were analyzed initially. Structured observation of Mr. Stebbin in these settings suggested specific instigating conditions as well as offering hypotheses about functions served by the SIBs. Initially, Mr. Stebbin was observed in transition to and from program activities attended by a large group of his peers. It was noted that in instances in which traffic became overly congested and/or excessively noisy, he became noticeably agitated as revealed by facial features, rapid body movements and arm flapping, and vocalizations. This pattern of responding suggested a state of anxiety or fearfulness. When displaying these agitation signs for a period of time exceeding 60 seconds or so, he was likely to engage in SIBs unless staff intervened and provided comforting physical touch and verbal reassurance. Occasionally under these conditions of arousal, peers bumped Mr. Stebbin and caused him to fall. On these instances, SIBs invariably occurred. In contrast, if bumped by peers when not in a state of anxious arousal, when with a staff member who immediately reassured him, or when in a quiet noncongested environment, Joel seldom engaged in SIBs.

Additionally, when in the hallway and approached by peers who were excessively noisy, he was prone to stop walking and cling onto the railing that he used for trailing. Again, facial features, motor activity, and vocalizations suggested increased personal distress, which if continued for over a minute was highly correlated with Mr. Stebbin's

SIBs.

Based on these observations, the diagnostic formulation was developed that Mr. Stebbin becomes fearful in noisy and traffic congested areas based on his history of being bumped or pushed by peers. This arousal state serves as a covert setting condition that renders him increasingly prone to engage in SIBs under the conditions of provocation such as being approached by a noisy peer or being bumped. Further, this state of arousal, if prolonged, appears to serve as a primary instigating condition.

The SIBs also occur in the context of a person with no functional communication skills, and no apparent skills of coping with the instigating conditions except through engaging in the SIBs. Additionally, the fear reaction occurs in a person with no functional vision who, as a result, is at a loss in interpreting various noises that appear to represent potential danger to him. He, it is assumed, feels unsafe when in noisy crowds based, as suggested, on his history of being pushed around by peers. These **tertiary** features, while having no direct instigating function, do contribute to Joel's reactions to various environmental stimuli.

Observation of Mr. Stebbin within the work activities program revealed that his SIBs were correlated with prompting from staff. In his new job placement, Mr. Stebbin was required to complete an easily accomplished but highly repetitive segment of an assembly line task within a specified period of time. Although the task was easily completed within the allotted period, Mr. Stebbin was prone, following a few initial minutes of continuous work, to pause for extended periods of time and engage in various stereotyped acts such as body-rocking or hand waving. During these times, he did not appear to be agitated. Rather, these forms of self-stimulation appeared to have more reinforcement value than that associated with the work activity. SIBs were likely to occur following prompting by staff to maintain a steady work pace. It also was noted that staff seldom interacted with Joel except when prompting him or to manage his SIBs. Finally, it was noted that Joel was provided a pay check at the end of each week, with the amount based on his productivity. This pay system appeared to be too abstract and delayed to serve as effective incentives for work activities. There were no other reinforcement contingencies associated with working. In sum, the primary instigating condition for the SIBs in the work activities program was the staff prompting. During the work period, SIBs invariably were preceded by staff prompts to return to his work. The secondary instigating condition was hypothesized to be the boring nature of the task and both the type and schedule of reinforcement. Tertiary factors were assumed to be the communication deficits, absence of vision, and those associated with Joel's motivational structure. Joel appeared to value self-initiated sensory stimulation and to demonstrate an underdeveloped work-related motivational structure. He had no alternative means of expressing his displeasure with the work task, staff prompting, or interruption of his self-stimulation except through his SIBs.

In sum, the hypothesized instigating conditions are as follows:

Primary: Being bumped by peer,
                  Being approached by a noisy peer,
                  State of anxious arousal exceeding one minute,
                  Staff prompting to continue work activity.

Secondary: Anxious arousal,
                  Large groups,
                  Noisy environment,
                  Boring nature of work task,
                  Schedule and type of reinforcement.

Tertiary :   Absence of communication skills,
                  Absence of arousal reduction skills,
                  Absence of vision,
                  Motivational features.

Diagnostic Formulations: Maintaining Conditions

Observational data support the hypothesis, based initially on information included on the data recording card, that when Joel was in, and during transition to and from, large groups the SIBs served two primary functions. Whenever he engages in SIBs, staff response is immediate. If he falls to the floor, staff immediately come to Joel's rescue and typically escort him to a program or living area location. If his SIBs are connected with his clinging to the railing, staff immediately offer him encouragement through taking him by the arm and guiding him to his destination. Thus, the distress-arousing condition is terminated and additionally, valued staff assistance is provided. In sum, Joel's SIBs are **functional**, it is reasoned, as these serve as a means of communicating his distress and, in so doing, to remove/reduce the personal distress and to gain staff assistance. The SIBs are assumed to be maintained primarily by negative reinforcement (distress reduction) and secondarily by positive reinforcement (valued social attention obtained).

Following SIBs in the work setting that were not terminated by staff verbal directives, it was observed that Mr. Stebbin would be removed from the assembly line and permitted to sit by himself until he chose to return or until the work period was over. He frequently would continue his stereotyped behaviors during this period. The SIBs, in this instance, appear to be functional in removing him from (a) the activity that apparently is a low preference one for him, and (b) the unpleasant prompting from staff. Further, these are followed by periods of time during which he can engage in uninterrupted episodes of self-stimulatory acts.

Diagnostically-Based Intervention

These diagnostic formulations were translated initially into a set of proactive behavior management interventions and staged to begin immediately. As initial management approaches, Mr. Stebbin was scheduled to leave program areas just prior to his peers to avoid congestion and excessive noise. He also was accompanied by staff to and from locations in which congestion and excessive noise were likely. During these periods, staff merely made their presence known and reassured him that they were available if he needed assistance or became fearful. As a result of these management approaches, the motivation underlying the SIBs was reduced/minimized. The SIBs reduced in frequency as instigating aversive conditions were reduced.

In an attempt to provide a functional alternative to Joel's

agitated vocalizations, arm flapping, and SIBs under arousal conditions, Joel was provided a program designed to teach the functional communication sign "Help Me". This program began after initial success with the management procedures. A more extensive communication training program became a continuing part of his active treatment experience. As a second treatment component, Joel was provided a relaxation training program initially, and later, after acquiring cue-controlled relaxation skills, was gradually exposed to noisy and congested environments. This program component was offered as a means of desensitizing him to those arousal-producing conditions that are inevitable components of this program environment.

As a means of increasing Joel's motivation to engage in work and as a replacement for the presumed automatic reinforcement associated with the body rocking and hand waving, Joel initially was provided a more challenging work activity involving both gross and fine arm-hand motor activity. Secondly, Joel was provided a token reinforcement program which involved self-delivery of a token reinforcer following completion of a specified set of work tasks. Joel was able to exchange tokens earned for purchases during break and following work, and to save for delayed but desired events such as purchasing a new music tape. He also was provided frequent praise for work behaviors. Finally, Joel's communication training program included teaching signs for "break" and "help me". He was provided the option of taking a break at any time if he wished to engage in stereotyped behaviors in a location away from the work station. However, Joel worked under the contingency that tokens and their valued back-up reinforcers could only be earned for work production. As these reinforcers became increasingly valuable to him, remaining in work activity became a predominate choice.

CASE 2

William Smith is a 22-year-old man with mild developmental disabilities who intermittently becomes physi-

cally aggressive and engages in episodes of self-injurious behaviors and urinary incontinence at both residential and vocational locations. He is being considered for placement in more independent living and work settings but the case manager is hesitant about these moves due to Mr. Smith's inclination to exhibit increased problem behaviors whenever his routine is disrupted.

The problem behaviors have been present since childhood and have been a major issue because he has required restrictive living arrangements and day programs to control his aggressive and self-injurious behaviors. At age 19, he was hospitalized following a major and prolonged aggressive and self-injurious episode that resulted in injury to staff. He was discharged to live in his current group home specializing in the management of persons with behavior disorders.

Mr. Smith is in good health. He has a history of generalized tonic-clonic seizures. His first one occurred when he was 18-months old, but with anticonvulsant therapy, his seizure disorder has been in remission for 5 years. His elongated facial structure and long limbs had suggested to some physicians that he might be suffering from some type of genetic disorder. He has four siblings, two of whom are developmentally disabled.

Mr. Smith was referred to a developmental disabilities diagnostic clinic for comprehensive diagnosis and treatment planning. At the time of referral, Mr. Smith/s drug regimen included: phenytoin (Dilantin) 200 mg x2/day (blood level - 15 mg/L), haloperidol (Haldol) 10 mg x2/day, and sertraline (Zoloft) 150 mg at bedtime.

Initial Data Collection

During the initial intake staffing, the clinic psychiatrist and psychologist met with the case manager and staff from the group home and vocational center and identified the following target behaviors as requiring complete functional analysis:

- Physical aggression,
- SIBs,
- Incontinence,
- Anxiety episodes (arm flapping, pacing, anxious facial expression), and
- Attention difficulties.

Following definition of each target problem, staff in both residential and vocational settings completed a data card (see Table 9.1) on each occurrence of physical aggression, SIBs, and incontinence. Anxiety episodes were evaluated through use of a rating scale developed to reflect the presence-absence of two or more of the symptoms (i.e., arm flapping, pacing, anxious facial expression) within each 30-minute period throughout the day. Additionally, on each occurrence of SIBs, physical aggression, or incontinence, staff was asked to note in the Other Observation section of the data card the presence/absence of an anxiety episode. Production rate in the vocational program was recorded at 30-minute intervals to provide a measure of attention difficulties.

The psychiatrist and psychologist of the diagnostic center continued to work closely with the case manager and staff of the group home and vocational center in devising, implementing, and monitoring a Multimodal Integrated Intervention Plan for Mr. Smith.

Medical Diagnostic-Intervention Formulations

Medical staff of the diagnostic clinic was asked to determine the possible effects of the seizure disorder and related medication regimen on the target symptoms. Additionally, an evaluation of a possible medical basis for the incontinence was requested. Finally, a genetic evaluation was sought to assess the presence of a genetic disorder that may contribute to the target symptoms and/or provide direction to an intervention program.

Results of the medical (general physical, neurological, and genetic) evaluations were as follows.

- The seizure medication was deemed appropriate and not considered to influence Mr. Smith's current behavior problems.

- Medical examination did not reveal a physical basis for the incontinence.

- A chromosome analysis suggested a diagnosis of fragile X syndrome. The functional implications of this diagnosis are discussed in the following psychiatry section.

In sum, with the exception of the potential influence of the fragile X syndrome, no medical basis was hypothesized as being related to the instigation or repeated occurrence of the target symptoms.

Psychiatric Diagnostic-Intervention Formulations

Diagnostic Formulations: Instigating Conditions

In presenting the psychiatric diagnostic formulations, the psychiatrist suggested that emotional lability, an inclination to react with a heightened level of arousal/anxiety, and attention difficulties are frequent features of the fragile X syndrome. Although not directly producing the target symptoms, this tertiary instigating influence suggests that Mr. Smith is prone to heightened affective arousal under stressful conditions and further is likely to experience difficulties with tasks that require focused attention for prolonged periods.

Mr. Smith's emotional features did meet the diagnostic criteria for a generalized anxiety disorder (see Table 9.2 for the DSM-III-R criteria and the functional equivalents presented by Mr. Smith):

Axis I. generalized anxiety disorder
Axis II. mild mental retardation
Axis III. fragile X syndrome.

TABLE 9.2 GENERALIZED ANXIETY DISORDER

DSM-III-R Criteria	Functional equivalent
A) unrealistic or excessive anxiety or worry	• has highly anxious facial expressions
B) anxiety unrelated to a mood disorder	• no evidence of mood disorder
C) at least 6/18 symptoms	
Motor Tension	
1) trembling/shaky	• appears tremulous
2) muscle tension	not present
3) restlessness	• paces when anxious
4) easy fatigability	not present
Vigilance/Scanning	
5) feeling keyed up/on edge	• hand flapping in anxiety provoking situations
6) exaggerated startle response	• aggressive behavior
7) difficulty concentrating	• highly distractible
Automatic Hyperactivity	
8) trouble falling/staying asleep	not present
9) irritability	not present
10) shortness of breath/feeling smothered	not present
11) palpitations/increased heart rate	not present
12) sweating/cold clammy hands	not present
13) dry mouth	not present
14) dizziness/lightheadedness	not present
15) nausea/diarrhea, abdominal distress	not present
16) hot flashes/chills	not present
17) frequent urination	• urinary incontinence
18) trouble swallowing/a lump in throat	not present

The anxious arousal was suggested as a significant secondary instigating event involved in the aggression, self-injury, and incontinence. There were no symptom patterns that suggested the presence of a major psychiatric disorder involving psychosis or depression. This latter diagnostic impression was needed in view of the current medications being prescribed for Mr. Smith.

In sum, the hypothesized instigating conditions are as follows:

Primary: None

Secondary: Anxious arousal

Tertiary: Fragile X syndrome
Generalized anxiety disorder.

Diagnostic Formulations: Maintaining Conditions

Reduction of distressful levels of arousal following occurrence of aggression, SIBs, and/or incontinence was hypothesized to contribute to the functionality of these symptoms.

Diagnostically-Based Psychiatric Interventions

To remove or minimize the state of distressful arousal presumed to serve as a secondary instigating condition, the following were recommended:

- The haloperidol be tapered off (because there was no indication for treatment with this drug).

- Then the sertraline be tapered off (because there was no indication for treatment with this drug).

- Buspirone, a novel anti-anxiety drug, would then be initiated. Drug dose would be started at 2.5 mg three times per day for 3 days to screen for sensitivity to side-effects. The daily dose would then be increased every 14 days - 5 mg three times per day, 10 mg three times per day, and then 15 mg three times per day. Medication effects on the target symptoms will be used to determine the most efficacious drug dose.

Psychological and Socioenvironmental Diagnostic-Intervention Formulations

Analysis of data obtained from the data cards completed by residental and vocational staff was followed by structured observations in both settings. This analysis resulted in the following psychosocial diagnostic formulations involving instigating and maintaining influences.

Diagnostic Formulations: Instigating Conditions

Each occurrence of aggression, SIBs, and incontinence was preceded by one of the following primary instigating events: (a) instructional demands, (b) sudden increase in ambient noise level, (c) disagreement with peer, and (d) sudden or previously unannounced changes in routine. Anxious arousal level frequently was noted to precede and/or occur simultaneously with aggression, SIBs, and incontinence, and is presumed to serve as a significant secondary instigating condition. Further, it was noted that aggression most frequently occurred as the final behavior in a chain, viz., arousal, hand waving/pacing, SIBs, and then aggression. If the source of provocation can be removed earlier in the chain, aggression on most occasions can be avoided.

There was a noticeable absence of skills of (a) coping with the various external sources of provocation except through use of the target symptoms and (b) identifying or self-managing the excessive overarousal. Thus, the lack of prosocial skills of coping with these primary and secondary instigating conditions is viewed as a significant tertiary instigating influence.

In sum, the hypothesized instigating conditions are as follows:

Primary: Instructional demands
                   Sudden increase in ambient noise level
                   Disagreement with peers
                   Sudden or previously unannounced changes
                   in routine.

Secondary: Anxious arousal.

Tertiary: Limited coping and anxiety management skills.

Diagnostic Formulations: Maintaining Conditions

Aggression, SIBs, and incontinence frequently were followed by removal from or reduction in the instigating conditions, that is, those that most typically resulted in noticeable arousal. Following removal or reduction of these sources of provocation, anxious arousal was reduced. Thus, it is hypothesized that these aberrant behaviors are functional as means of escape from aversive conditions.

Diagnostically-Based Psychosocial Interventions

The following *proactive and reactive behavior management* procedures were recommended as means of reducing the instigating conditions:

- Provide choices whenever possible, especially in those situations in which Mr. Smith is prone to excessive arousal,

- Provide lead time. Prepare Mr. Smith for any changes in his routine.

- Maintain ambient noise at a low level whenever possible. Provide Mr. Smith a choice of leaving the environment if it becomes uncomfortable to him.

- Prompt a calming response or redirect Mr. Smith whenever he begins waving his hands or pacing. Attempt to identify the source of provocation and remove/reduce it. Reduction of arousal level at this point may avoid SIBs and aggression.

Following initiation of these behavior management procedures, provide specific coping, including anxiety management, skills training in alternative ways of responding both to the sources of provocation as well as to the anxious arousal itself.

To increase attention and persistence to task, provide a choice of work activities. Provide training in self-management, including self-delivery of token reinforcers on attainment of work performance criteria. This training will provide Mr. Smith with skills of focusing his attention to the task at hand and of self-managing the contingencies present in the work environment.

Staging of Interventions

As noted earlier, multicomponent interventions should be staged sequentially in order to evaluate the specific and relative effects of each. This is of especial significance whenever drug or other interventions are used that have potential negative side effects or that require significant investment of resources to implement and maintain. In completing the initial Multimodal Integrated Intervention Plan for Mr. Smith, the team decided to evaluate the effects of the withdrawal of the haloperidol and sertraline followed by initiation of buspirone. No changes in staff approaches to relating to Mr. Smith or his target symptoms were made during this initial intervention phase.

Maximum effect on the anxiety episodes (arm flapping, pacing), attention difficulties (production rate in vocational program), and on the remaining targets of SIBs, aggression, and incontinence were obtained at the dose level of 10 mg three times per day. This drug regimen was maintained as the behavior management procedures were initiated. Following staff training in use of these routines, the treatment components of the psychosocial program were begun. As a basis for ongoing evaluation of program effectiveness, data collection was continued as each phase was added.

Mr. Smith currently is participating successfully in a coping skills training program and has demonstrated success in spontaneous use of these skills in both work and group home settings. Target symptoms continue to occur, although with significantly reduced frequency and severity. Each incident is evaluated by staff in an ongoing effort to provide more effective program experiences for Mr. Smith. The case manager, in regular consultation with the clinic staff, has begun the process of placement of Mr. Smith in more independent living and vocational settings. The team has decided to continue the medication and components of the psychosocial interventions during transition to these new placements. If successful in this transition without a significant recurrence of target symptoms, drug tapering will be considered.

Summary

These case studies illustrate the steps involved from observation to diagnostic formulations as these are translated into management and treatment interventions. As these interventions are implemented, staff continues to complete a behavior recording form on each target symptom. Additionally, data are obtained on occurrence of replacment skills such as the use of functional signing, coping with instigating conditions, amount of time spent in work, and number of tokens earned.

These ongoing data gathering and analysis activities provide a means of evaluating the efficacy of the interventions as well as the utility in reducing the target symptoms of the underlying hypotheses about instigating and maintaining conditions. Effective procedures are continued. Ineffective ones are discarded and replaced by others. In sum, the diagnostic-intervention formulation process is an ongoing one and continues until the problem behaviors are eliminated and replaced by acceptable functional alternatives.

REFERENCES AND SUGGESTED READINGS

Altman, K., Haavik, S., & Cook, J. W. (1978). Punishment of self-injurious behavior in natural settings using contingent aromatic ammonia. **Behaviour Research and Therapy, 16**, 85-96.

American Psychiatric Association. (1987). **Diagnostic and statistical manual of mental disorders, Third Edition - Revised.** Washington, DC: American Psychiatric Association.

Azrin, N. H., Besalel, V. A., Jamner, J. P., & Caputo, J. N. (1988). Comparative study of behavioral methods of treating severe self-injury. **Residential Behavioral Treatment, 3**, 119-152.

Azrin, N. H., Besalel, V. A., & Wisotzek, I. E. (1982). Treatment of self-injury by a reinforcement plus interruption procedure. **Analysis and Intervention in Developmental Disabilities, 3**, 105-113.

Azrin, N. H., Gottlieb, L., Hughart, L., Wesolowski, M. D., & Rahn, T. (1975). Eliminating self-injurious behavior by educative procedures. **Behaviour Research and Therapy, 13**, 101-111.

Baron-Cohen, S. (1989). Do autistic children have obsessions and compulsions? **British Journal of Clinical Psychology, 28**, 193-200.

Barron, B., & Sandman, C. A. (1984). Self-injurious behavior and stereotypy in an institutionalized mentally retarded population. **Applied Research in Mental Retardation, 5**, 499-511.

Barron, J., & Sandman, C. A. (1985). Paradoxical excitement to sedative-hypnotics in mentally retarded clients. **American Journal of Mental Deficiency, 90**, 124-129.

Baumeister, A. A., & MacLean, W. E., Jr. (1984). Deceleration of self-injurious and stereotypic responding by exercise. **Applied Research in Mental Retardation, 5**, 385-393.

Baumeister, A. A., & Rollings, J. P. (1976). Self-injurious behavior. In N. R. Ellis (Ed.), **International review of research in mental retardation** (Vol. 8, pp. 1-34). New York: Academic Press.

Baumeister, A. A., & Sevin, J. A. (1990). Pharmacologic control of aberrant behavior in the mentally retarded: Toward a more rational approach. **Neuroscience & Biobehavioral Reviews, 14**, 253-262.

Bird, F., Dores, P. A., Moniz, D., & Robinson, J. (1989). Reducing severe aggressive and self-injurious behaviors with functional communication training. **American Journal of Mental Retardation, 94**, 37-48.

Blankenship, M. D., & Lamberts, F. (1989). Helmet restraint and visual screening as treatment for self-injurious behavior in persons who have profound mental retardation. **Behavioral Residential Treatment**, 4, 253-265.

Borreson, P. M. (1980). The elimination of self-injury avoidance responding through a forced running consequence. **Mental Retardation, 18**, 73-77.

Burd, L., Fisher, W., Kerbeshian, J., & Arnold, M. E. (1987). Is the development of Tourette disorder a marker for improvements of patients with autism and other pervasive developmental disorders? **Journal of the American Academy of Child and Adolescent Psychiatry, 26**, 162-165.

Burke, M. M., Burke, D., & Forehand, R. (1985). Interpersonal antecedents of self-injurious behavior in retarded children. **Education and Training of the Mentally Retarded, 20**, 204-208.

Butterfield, W. H. (1975). Electric shock -- Safety factors when used for the aversive conditioning of humans. **Behavior Therapy, 6**, 98-110.

Carr, E. G. (1977). The motivation of self-injurious behavior: A review of some hypotheses. **Psychological Bulletin, 84,** 800-816.

Carr, E. (1988). Functional equivalence as a mechanism of response generalization. In R. Horner, R. Koegel, & G. Dunlap (Eds.), **Generalization and maintenance: Life-style changes in applied settings** (pp. 221-241). Baltimore: Paul H. Brookes.

Carr, E. G., & Carlson, J. I. (1993). Reduction of severe behavior problems in the community using a multicomponent treatment approach. **Journal of Applied Behavior Analysis, 26,** 157-172.

Carr, E. G., & Durand, V. M. (1985). Reducing behavior problems through functional communication training. **Journal of Applied Behavior Analysis, 18,** 111-126.

Carr, E. G., Levin, L., McConnachie, G., Carlson, J., Kemp, D. C., & Smith, C. E. (1994). **Communication-based intervention for problem behavior.** Baltimore: Paul H. Brookes Publishing.

Carr, E. G., Newsom, C. D., & Binkoff, J. A. (1976). Stimulus control of self-destructive behavior in a psychotic child. **Journal of Abnormal Child Psychology, 4,** 139-153.

Cataldo, M. F., & Harris, J. (1982). The biological basis for self-injury in the mentally retarded. **Analysis and Intervention in Developmental Disabilities, 2,** 21-39.

Cowery, G. E., Iwata, B. A., & Pace, G. M. (1990). Effects and side effects of DRO as treatment of self-injurious behavior. **Journal of Applied Behavior Analysis, 23,** 497-506.

Day, R., Rea, J., Schuster, N., Larsen, S., & Johnson, W. (1988). A functionally based approach to the treatment of self-injurious behavior. **Behavior Modification, 12,** 565-589.

de Catanzaro, D. A., & Baldwin, G. (1978). Effective treatment of self-injurious behavior through a forced arm exercise. **American Journal of Mental Deficiency, 82,** 433-439.

Dorsey, M. F., Iwata, B. A., Ong, P., & McSween, T. E. (1980). Treatment of self-injurious behavior using a water mist: Initial response suppression and generalization. **Journal of Applied Behavior Analysis, 13,** 343-353.

Duker, P. C. (1988). **Teaching the developmentally handicapped communicative gesturing.** Berwyn, PA: Swets, N. America Inc.

Duker, P., Jol, K., & Palmen, A. (1991). The collateral decrease of self-injurious behavior with teaching communicative gestures to individuals who are mentally retarded. **Behavioral Residential Treatment, 6,** 183-196.

Durand, V. M. (1990). **Severe behavior problems: a functional communication training approach.** New York: Guilford Press.

Durand, V. M., & Carr, E. G. (1987). Social influences on "self-stimulatory" behavior: Analysis and treatment application. **Journal of Applied Behavior Analysis, 20,** 119-132.

Durand, V. M., & Carr, E. G. (1991). Functional communication training to reduce challenging behaviors: Maintenance and application in new settings. **Journal of Applied Behavior Analysis, 24,** 251-264.

Durand, V. M., & Crimmins, D. B. (1988). Identifying the variables maintaining self-injurious behavior. **Journal of Autism and Developmental Disorders, 18,** 99-117.

Durand, V. M., Crimmins, D. B., Caufield, M., & Taylor, J. (1989). Reinforcer assessment I: Using problem behavior to select reinforcers. **Journal of the Association for Persons with Severe Handicaps, 114,** 113-126.

Durand, V. M., & Kishi, G. (1987). Reducing severe behavior problems among persons with dual sensory impairments: An evaluation of a technical assistance model. **JASH, 12,** 2-10.

Edelson, S. M. (1984). Implications of sensory stimulation in self-destructive behavior. **American Journal of Mental Deficiency, 89,** 140-145.

Edelson, S. M., Taubman, M. T., & Lovaas, I. (1983). Some social contexts of self-destructive behavior. **Journal of Abnormal Child Psychology, 11**, 299-312.

Farber, J. M. (1987). Psychopharmacology of self-injurious behavior in the mentally retarded. **Journal of the American Academy of Child and Adolescent Psychiatry, 26**, 296-302.

Favell, J. E., (Task Force Chairperson) (1982). The treatment of self-injurious behavior. **Behavior Therapy, 13**, 529-554.

Favell, J. E., McGimsey, J. F., & Schnell, R. M. (1982). Treatment of self-injury by providing alternate sensory activities. **Analysis and Intervention in Developmental Disabilities, 2**, 83-104.

Fenwick, P. (1989). The nature and management of aggression in epilepsy. **Journal of Neuropsychiatry, 1**, 418-425.

Fisher, W., Piazza, C., Cataldo, M., Harrell, R., Jefferson, G., & Conner, R. (1993). Functional communication training with and without extinction and punishment. **Journal of Applied Behavior Analysis, 26**, 23-36.

Foxx, R. M. (1990). "Harry": A ten year follow-up of the successful treatment of a self-injurious man. **Research in Developmental Disabilities, 11**, 67-76.

Foxx, R. M., & Bechtel, D. R. (1983). Overcorrection: A review and analysis. In S. Axelrod & J. Apsche (Eds.), **The effects of punishment on human behavior** (pp. 227-288). New York: Academic Press.

Gardner, D. L., & Cowdry, R. W. (1985). Suicidal and parasuicidal behavior in borderline personality disorders. **Psychiatric Clinic North America, 8**, 389-403.

Gardner, W. I., Cole, C. L., Davidson, D. P., & Karan, O. C. (1986). Reducing aggression in individuals with developmental disabilities: An expanded stimulus control, assessment, and intervention model. **Education and Training of the Mentally Retarded, 21**, 3-12.

Gardos, G., Cole, J. O., & Tarsy, D. (1978). Withdrawal syndromes associated with antipsychotic drugs. **American Journal of Psychiatry, 135**, 1321-1324.

Gedye, A. (1989). Extreme self-injury attributed to frontal lobe seizures. **American Journal of Mental Retardation, 94**, 20-26.

Gedye, A. (1990). Dietary increase in serotonin reduces self-injurious behavior in a Down's syndrome adult. **Journal of Mental Deficiency Research, 34**, 195-203.

Gedye, A. (1991). Tourette syndrome attributed to frontal lobe dysfunction: Numerous etiologies involved. **Journal of Clinical Psychology, 47**, 233-252.

Gedye, A. (1992). Serotonin-GABA treatment is hypothesized for self-injury in Lesch-Nyhan syndrome. **Medical Hypotheses, 38**, 325-328.

Glennon, R. A. (1990). Serotonin receptors: Clinical implications. **Neuroscience Biobehavioral Reviews, 14**, 35-47.

Goldstein, M., Anderson, L. T., Reuben, R., & Dancis, J. (1985). Self-mutilation in Lesch-Nyhan disease is caused by dopaminergic denervation. **The Lancet, 1**, 338-339.

Grace, N., Cowart, C., & Matson, J. L. (1988). Reinforcement and self-control for treating a chronic case of self-injury in Lesch-Nyhan syndrome. **Journal of the Multihandicapped Person, 1**, 53-59.

Greene, R. J., & Hoats, D. L. (1971). Aversive tickling: A simple conditioning technique. **Behavior Therapy, 2**, 389-393.

Gualtieri, C. T. (1989). The differential diagnosis of self-injurious behavior in mentally retarded people. **Psychopharmacology Bulletin, 25,** 358-363.

Gualtieri, C. T., & Schroeder, S. R. (1989). Pharmacotherapy for self-injurious behavior: Preliminary tests of the D^1 hypothesis. **Psychopharmacology Bulletin, 25,** 364-371.

Gualtieri, C. T., Sovner, R. (1989). Akathisia and tardive akathisia. **Psychiatric Aspects of Mental Retardation Reviews, 8,** 83-88.

Guess, D., & Carr, D. (1991). Emergence and maintenance of stereotypy and self-injury. **American Journal of Mental Retardation, 96,** 299-320.

Gunsett, R. P., Mulick, J. A., Fernald, W. B., & Martin, J. L. (1989). Indications for medical screening prior to behavioral programming for severely and profoundly mentally retarded clients. **Journal of Autism and Developmental Disorders, 19,** 167-172.

Hamilton, H., Stephens, L., & Allen, P. (1967). Controlling aggressive and destructive behavior in severely retarded institutionalized residents. **American Journal of Mental Deficiency, 71,** 852-856.

Hamilton, M. S., & Opler, L. A. (1992). Akathisia, suicidality, and fluoxetine. **Journal of Clinical Psychiatry, 53,** 401-406.

Harris, J. C. (1992). Neurobiological factors in self-injurious behavior. In J. K. Luiselli, J. L. Matson, & N. Singh (Eds.), **Self-injurious behavior: Analysis, assessment, and treatment** (pp. 59-150). New York: Springer-Verlag.

Harris, S. L., & Romanczyk, R. G. (1976). Treating self-injurious behavior of a retarded child by overcorrection. **Behavior Therapy, 7,** 235-239.

Heidorn, S. D., & Jensen, C. C. (1984). Generalization and maintenance of the reduction of self-injurious behaviors maintained by 2
types of reinforcement. **Behavior Research and Therapy, 22,**
581-586.

Hermann, B. H. (1991). Effects of opioid receptors in the treatment of
autism and self-injurious behavior. In J. J. Ratey (Ed.), **Mental
retardation: developing pharmacotherapies** (pp. 107-137).
Washington, DC: American Psychiatric Press.

Holburn, C. S. (1986). Aerophagia: An uncommon form of self-injury.
American Journal of Mental Deficiency, 91, 201-203.

Holburn, C. S., & Dougher, M. J. (1985). Behavioral attempts to
eliminate air-swallowing in two profoundly mentally retarded clients. **American Journal of Mental Deficiency, 89,** 524-536.

Holburn, C. S., & Dougher, M. (1986). Effects of response satiation
procedures in the treatment of aerophogia. **American Journal of
Mental Deficiency, 91,** 72-77.

Horner, R. (1980). The effects of an environmental "enrichment"
program on the behavior of institutionalized profoundly retarded
children. **Journal of Applied Behavior Analysis, 13,** 473-491.

Horner, R. H., & Budd, C. M. (1985). Acquisition of manual sign use:
Collateral reduction of maladaptive behavior, and factors limiting
generalization. **Education and Training of the Mentally Retarded, 20,** 39-47.

Horner, R. H., & Day, H. M. (1991). The effects of response efficiency
on functionally equivalent competing behaviors. **Journal of Applied Behavior Analysis, 24,** 719-732.

Horner, R. H., Day, H. M., Sprague, J. R., O'Brien, M., & Heathfield, L.
T. (1991). Interspersed requests: A nonaversive procedure for
decreasing aggression and self-injury during instruction. **Journal
of Applied Behavior Analysis, 24,** 265-278.

Hurley, A. D., & Sovner, R. (1991). Attention deficit-hyperactivity disorder. **Habilitative Mental Healthcare Newsletter, 10,** 19-24.

Isley, E. M., Kartsonis, C., McCurley, C. M., Weisz, K. E. & Roberts, M. S. (1991). Self-restraint: A review of etiology and applications in mentally retarded adults with self-injury. **Research in Developmental Disabilities, 12,** 87-95.

Iwata, B. A., Dorsey, M. F., Slifer, K. J., Bauman, K. E., & Richman, G. S. (1982). Toward a functional analysis of self-injury. **Analysis and Intervention in Developmental Disabilities, 2,** 3-20.

Iwata, B. A., Pace, G. M., Kalsher, M. J., Cowdery, G. E., & Cataldo, M. F. (1990a). Experimental analysis and extinction of self-injurious escape behavior. **Journal of Applied Behavior Analysis, 23,** 11-27.

Iwata, B. A., Pace, G. M., Kissel, R. C., Nau, P. A., & Farber, J. M. (1990b). The Self-Injury Trauma (SIT) Scale: A method for quantifying surface tissue damage caused by self-injurious behavior. **Journal of Applied Behavior Analysis, 23,** 99-110.

Jacobs, B. L. (1991). Serotonin and behavior: Emphasis on motor control. **Journal of Clinical Psychiatry, 52** (12, suppl), 17-23.

Jaffe, J. H., & Martin, W. R. (1990). Opioid analgesics and antagonists. In A. Goodman Gilman, T. W. Rall, A. S. Nies, & P. Taylor (Eds.), **Goodman and Gilman's the pharmacological basis of therapeutics eighth edition** (pp. 485-521). New York: Pergamon Press.

Johnson, W. L., Baumeister, A. A., Penland, M. J., & Inwald, C. (1982). Experimental analysis of self-injurious, stereotypic, and collateral behavior of retarded persons: Effects of overcorrection and reinforcement of alternative responding. **Analysis and Intervention in Developmental Disabilities, 2,** 41-66.

Kendler, K. A. (1976). A medical student's experience with akathisia. **American Journal of Psychiatry, 133,** 454-455.

Kerbeshian, J., Burd, L. (1991). A clinical pharmacological approach to the treatment of autism. **Habilitative Mental Healthcare Newsletter, 10**, 33-36.

King, B. H. (1993). Self-injury by people with mental retardation: A compulsive behavior hypothesis. **American Journal of Mental Retardation, 98**, 93-112.

Kinsbourne, M. (1980). Do repetitive movement patterns in children and animals serve a dearousing function? **Developmental and Behavioral Pediatrics, 1**, 39-42.

Lancioni, G. E., Smeets, P. M., Ceccarani, P. S., Capodaglio, L., & Campanari, G. (1984). Effects of gross motor activities on the severe self-injurious tantrums of multihandicapped individuals. **Applied Research in Mental Retardation, 5,** 471-482.

Lechman, J. F., Walker, D. E., & Cohen, D. J. (1993). Premonitory urges in Tourette's syndrome. **American Journal of Psychiatry, 150,** 98-102.

Linscheid, T. R. (1992). Aversive stimulation. In J. K. Luiselli, J. L. Matson, & N. N. Singh, **Self-Injurious behavior: Analysis, assessment, and treatment** (pp. 269-292). New York: Springer-Verlag.

Linscheid, T. R., Iwata, B. A., Ricketts, R. W., Williams, D. E., & Griffin, J. C. (1990). Clinical evaluation of the self-injurious behavior inhibiting system (SIBIS). **Journal of Applied Behavior Analysis, 23,** 53-78.

Lockwood, K., & Bourland, G. (1982). Reduction of self-injurious behaviors by reinforcement and toy use. **Mental Retardation, 20,** 169-173.

Lovaas, O. I., Freitag, G., Gold, V., & Kassorla, I. (1965). Experimental studies in childhood schizophrenia: Analysis of self-destructive behavior. **Journal of Experimental Child Psychology, 2**, 67-84.

Lovaas, O. I., Newsom, C., & Hickman, C. (1987). Self-stimulatory behavior and perceptual reinforcement. **Journal of Applied Behavior Analysis, 20,** 45-68.

Lovaas, O. I., & Simmons, J. Q. (1969). Manipulation of self-destruction in three retarded children. **Journal of Applied Behavior Analysis, 2,** 143-157.

Lowry, M. A., & Sovner, R. (1991). The functional significance of problem behavior: A key to effective treatment. **The Habilitative Mental Healthcare Newsletter, 10,** 59-63.

Lowry, M. A., & Sovner, R. (1992). Severe behaviour problems associated with rapid cycling bipolar disorder in two adults with profound mental retardation. **Journal of Intellectual Disability Research, 36,** 269-281.

Lucero, W. J., Frieman, J., Spooring, K., & Fehrenbacher, J. (1976). Comparison of three procedures in reducing self-injurious behavior. **American Journal of Mental Deficiency, 80,** 548-554.

Luchins, D. J. (1990). A review of pharmacological agents for self-injurious behavior. **Progress in Neuro-Psychopharmacology & Biological Psychiatry, 14,** S169-S179.

Luchins, D. J., & Dojka, D. (1989). Lithium and propranolol in aggression and self-injurious behavior in the mentally retarded. **Psychopharmacological Bulletin, 25,** 372-375.

Luiselli, J. K. (1984). Therapeutic effects of brief contingent effort on severe behavior disorders in children with developmental disabilities. **Journal of Clinical Child Psychology, 13,** 257-262.

Luiselli, J. K. (1991). Functional assessment and treatment of self-injury in a pediatric, nursing-care resident. **Behavioral Residential Treatment, 6,** 311-319.

Luiselli, J. K., Matson, J. L., & Singh, N. (Eds.). (1992). **Self-Injurious behavior: Analysis, assessment, and treatment.** New York: Springer-Verlag.

Mace, F. C., Hock, M. L., Lalli, J. S., West, B. J., Belfiore, P., Pinter, E., & Brown, D. K. (1988). Behavioral momentum in the treatment of noncompliance. **Journal of Applied Behavior Analysis, 21,** 123-141.

Mace, F. C., Lalli, J. S., & Shea, M. C. (1992). Functional analysis and treatment of self-injury. In J. K. Luiselli, J. L. Matson, and N. N. Singh (Eds.), **Self-injurious behaviors: Analysis, assessment, and treatment** (pp. 122-152). New York: Springer-Verlag.

Markowitz, P. I. (1990). Fluoxetine treatment of self-injurious behavior in mentally retarded patients. **Journal of Clinical Psychopharmacology, 10,** 299-300.

Markowitz, P. I. (1992). Effect of fluoxetine on self-injurious behavior in the developmentally disabled; a preliminary study. **Journal of Clinical Psychopharmacology, 12,** 27-31.

Matson, J. L., & Keyes, J. B. (1990). A comparison of DRO to movement suppression time-out and DRO with two self-injurious and aggressive mentally retarded adults. **Research in Developmental Disabilities, 11,** 111-120.

McNally, R. J., Calamari, J. E., Hansen, P. M., & Kaliher, C. (1988). Behavioral treatment of psychogenic polydipsia. **Journal of Behavior Therapy and Experimental Psychiatry, 19,** 57-61.

Measel, C. J., & Alfieri, P. A. (1976). Treatment of self-injurious behavior by a combination of reinforcement for incompatible behavior and overcorrection. **American Journal of Mental Deficiency, 81,** 147-153.

Merbaum, M. (1973). The modification of self-destructive behavior by a mother-therapist using aversive stimulation. **Behavior Therapy, 4,** 442-447.

Miczek, K. A., Mos, J., & Olivier, B. (1989). Serotonin, aggression and self-destructive behavior. **Psychopharmacological Bulletin, 25,** 399-403.

Mikkelsen, E. J. (1986). Low-dose haloperidol for stereotypic self-injurious behavior in the mentally retarded. New England Journal of Medicine, 315, 398-399.

National Institutes of Health (1989). Consensus development conference statement on treatment of destructive behaviors in persons with developmental disabilities. Washington, DC: Author.

Oliver, C., & Head, D. (1990). Self-injurious behavior in people with learning disabilities: Determinants and interventions. International Review of Psychiatry, 2, 101-116.

Oliver, C., Murphy, G. H., & Corbett, J. A. (1987). Self-injurious behaviour in people with mental handicap: A total population study. Journal of Mental Deficiency Research, 31, 147-162.

O'Neill, R. E., Horner, R. H., Albin, R. W., Storey, K. & Sprague, J. R. (1990). Functional analysis of problem behavior. Sycamore Publishing: Sycamore, IL.

Osman, O. T., & Loschen, E. L. (1992). Self-injurious behavior in the developmentally disabled: pharmacologic treatment. Psychopharmacology Bulletin, 28, 439-449.

Pace, G. M., Iwata, B. A., Cowdery, G. E., Andree, P. J., & McIntyre, T. (1993). Stimulus (instructional) fading during extinction of self-injurious escape behavior. Journal of Applied Behavior Analysis, 26, 205-212.

Rapoff, M. A., Altman, K., & Christophersen, E. R. (1980). Reducing aggressive and self-injurious behavior in an institutionalized retarded blind child's self-hitting by response-contingent brief restraint. Education and Treatment of Children, 3, 231-236.

Ratey, J. J. (Ed.). (1991). Mental retardation: Developing pharmacotherapies. Washington, DC: American Psychiatric Press.

Ratey, J. J., Sovner, R., Mikkelsen, E., & Chmielinski, H. E. (1989). Buspirone therapy for maladaptive behavior and anxiety in developmentally disabled persons. **Journal of Clinical Psychiatry, 50,** 382-384.

Ratey, J. J., Sovner, R., Parks, A., & Rogentine, K. (1991). Buspirone treatment of aggression and anxiety in mentally retarded patients: A multiple-baseline, placebo lead-in study. **Journal of Clinical Psychiatry, 52,** 159-162.

Regain, R. D., & Anson, J. E. (1976). The control of self-mutilating behavior with positive reinforcement. **Mental Retardation, 14**(3), 22-25.

Reichie, J., & Wacker, D. (Eds.). (1993). **Communicative alternatives to challenging behaviors.** Baltimore: Paul H. Brookes Publishing.

Reid, A. H. (1982). **The psychiatry of mental handicap.** London: Blackwell Scientific Publications.

Reid, A. H. (1984). Gilles de la Tourette syndrome in mental handicap. **Journal of Mental Deficiency Research, 28,** 81-83.

Reid, A. H. (1989). Schizophrenia in mental retardation: Clinical features. **Research in Developmental Disabilities, 10,** 241-249.

Repp, A. C., & Singh, N. N. (Eds.). (1990). **Perspectives on the use of nonaversive and aversive intervention for persons with developmental disabilities.** Sycamore, IL: Sycamore Publishing.

Rincover, A., & Devany, J. (1982). The application of sensory extinction procedures to self-injury. **Analysis and Intervention in Developmental Disabilities, 2,** 67-81.

Robertson, M. M., Trimble, M. R., & Lees, A. J. (1989). Self-injurious behavior and the Gilles de la Tourette syndrome: A clinical study and review of the literature. **Psychological Medicine, 19,** 611-25.

Rohan, J. (1986). Self-injurious and stereotypic behavior of noninstitutionalized mentally retarded people: Prevalence and classification. **American Journal of Mental Deficiency, 91**, 268-276.

Rojahn, J., & Marshburn, E. C. (1992). Facial screening and visual occlusion. In J. K. Luiselli, J. L. Matson, & N. N. Singh (Eds.), **Self-injurious behaviors: Analysis, assessment, and treatment** (pp. 200-234). New York: Springer-Verlag.

Romanczyk, R. G. (1986). Self-injurious behavior: Conceptualization, assessment, and treatment. In K. Gadow (Ed.), **Advances in learning and behavioral disabilities,** (pp. 29-56). Greenwich, CT: JAI Press.

Romanczyk, R. G., & Goren, E. (1975). Self-injurious behavior: The problem of clinical control. **Journal of Clinical Psychology, 43,** 730-739.

Romanczyk, R. G., Lockshin, S., & O'Connor, J. (1992). Psycho-physiology and issues of anxiety and arousal. In J. K. Luiselli, J. L. Matson, & N. N. Singh (Eds.), **Self-injurious behaviors: Analysis, assessment, and treatment** (pp. 93-121). New York: Springer-Verlag.

Sandman, C. A. (1990/1991). The opiate hypothesis in autism and self-injury. **Journal of Child and Adolescent Psychopharmacology, 1,** 237-248.

Sanderman, C. A., Barron, J. L., Chicz-DeMet, A., & DeMet, E. M. (1990). Plasma B-endorphin levels in patients with self-injurious behavior and stereotypy. **American Journal of Mental Retardation, 95,** 84-92.

Saposnek, D. T., & Watson, L. S., Jr. (1974). The elimination of the self-destructive behavior of a psychotic child: A case study. **Behavior Therapy, 5,** 79-89.

Schroeder, S. R., & Luiselli, J. K. (1992). Self-restraint. In J. K. Luiselli, J. L. Matson, & N. N. Singh (Eds.), **Self-injurious behaviors: Analysis, assessment, and treatment** (pp. 293-306). New York: Springer-Verlag.

Schroeder, S. R., Peterson, C. R., Solomon, L. J., & Artley, J. J. (1977). EMG feedback and the contingent restraint of self-injurious behavior among the severely retarded: Two case illustrations. **Behavior Therapy, 8,** 738-741.

Schroeder, S. R., Rojahn, J., Mulick, J. A., & Schroeder, C. S. (1990). Self-injurious behavior. In J. L. Matson (Ed.), **Handbook of behavior modification with the mentally retarded** (2nd ed., pp. 141-180). New York; Plenum Press.

Singer, G. H., Singer, J., & Horner, R. H. (1987). Using pretask requests to increase the probability of compliance for students with severe disabilities. **Journal of the Association for Persons with Severe Handicaps, 12,** 287-291.

Singh, N. N., & Millichamp, C. J. (1985). Pharmacological treatment of self-injurious behavior in mentally retarded persons. **Journal of Autism and Developmental Disorders, 15,** 257-267.

Smith, R. G., Iwata, B. A., Vollmer, T. R., & Zarcone, J. R. (1993). Experimental analysis and treatment of multiply controlled self-injury. **Journal of Applied Behavior Analysis, 26,** 183-196.

Solnick, J. V., Rincover, A., & Peterson, C. R. (1977). Some determinants of the reinforcing and punishing effects of timeout. **Journal of Applied Behavior Analysis, 10,** 415-424.

Sovner, R. (1986). Limiting factors in the use of DSM-III with mentally ill/mentally retarded persons. **Psychopharmacology Bulletin, 22,** 1055-1059.

Sovner, R. (1991). The treatment of neuro-psychiatric disorders in developmentally disabled persons with anticonvulsant drug therapy. In J. J. Ratey (Ed.), **Mental retardation: emerging pharmacotherapies** (pp. 83-106). Washington DC: American Psychiatric Press.

Sovner, R., Fox, C. J., Lowry, M. J., & Lowry, M. A. (1993). Fluoxetine treatment of self-injury and depression in two adults with mental retardation. **Journal of Intellectual Disability, 37**, 301-311.

Sovner, R., & Hurley, A. D. (1985). Assessing the quality of psychotropic drug regimens prescribed for mentally retarded persons. **Psychiatric Aspects of Mental Retardation Reviews, 4**, 31-38.

Sovner, R., & Hurley, A. D. (1986). Managing aggressive behavior: A psychiatric approach. **Psychiatric Aspects of Mental Retardation Reviews, 5**, 16-21.

Sovner, R., & Hurley, A. D. (1992). The diagnostic treatment formulation for psychotropic drug therapy. **The Habilitative Mental Healthcare Newsletter, 11**, 81-86.

Sovner, R., & Lowry, M. A. (in press). A psychotropic drug therapy paradigm for the management of maladaptive behavior associated with organic mental syndromes. In A. Dosen & K. Day (Eds.), **The treatment of mental illness and behavior disorders in mentally retarded children and adults.**

Sovner, R., & Pary, R. J. (1993). Affective disorders in developmentally disabled persons. In J. L. Matson & R. P. Barrett (Eds.), **Psychopathology in the mentally retarded** (pp. 87-147). Boston: Allyn and Bacon.

Stahl, S. (1992). Serotonin neuroscience discoveries usher in a new era of novel drug therapies for psychiatry. **Psychopharmacological Bulletin, 28**, 3-9.

Steege, M. W., Wacker, D. P., Berg, W. K., Cigrand, K. K., & Cooper, L. J. (1989). The use of behavioral assessment to prescribe and evaluate treatment for severely handicapped children. **Journal of Applied Behavior Analysis, 22,** 22-23.

Steen, P. L., & Zuriff, G. E. (1977). The use of relaxation in the treatment of self-injurious behavior. **Journal of Behavior Therapy and Experimental Psychiatry, 8,** 447-448.

Steingard, R. & Biederman, J. (1987). Lithium responsive manic-like symptoms in two individuals with autism and mental retardation. **Journal of the American Academy of Child and Adolescent Psychiatry, 27,** 932-935.

Szymanski, L. S., Rubin, I. L. & Tarjan, G. (1989). Mental retardation. In A. Tasman, R. E. Hales, & A. J. Frances (Eds.), **American Psychiatric Press Review of Psychiatry** (pp. 217-239). Washington, DC: American Psychiatric Press.

Tarpley, H. D., & Schroeder, S. R. (1979). Comparison of DRO and DRI on rate of suppression of self-injurious behavior. **American Journal of Mental Deficiency, 84,** 188-194.

Tate, B. G., & Baroff, G. S. (1966). Aversive control of self-injurious behavior in a psychotic boy. **Behaviour Research and Therapy, 4,** 281-287.

Tierney, D. W. (1986). The reinforcement of calm sitting behavior: A method used to reduce the self-injurious behavior of a profoundly retarded boy. **Journal of Behavior Therapy and Experimental Psychiatry, 17,** 47-50.

Thompson, T., Axtell, S., & Schaal, D. (1993). Self-injurious behavior: mechanisms and interventions. In J. L. Matson & R. P. Barrett (Eds.), **Psychopathology in the mentally retarded** (pp. 179-211). Needham Heights, MA: Allyn and Bacon.

Touchette, P. E., MacDonald, R. F., & Langer, S. N. (1985). A scatter plot for identifying stimulus control of problem behavior. **Journal of Applied Behavior Analysis, 18,** 343-351.

Tranebjaerg, L., & Orum, A. (1991). Major depressive disorder as a prominent but underestimated feature of fragile x syndrome. **Comprehensive Psychiatry, 32,** 83-87.

Turk, J. (1992). The fragile x syndrome. **British Journal of Psychiatry, 160,** 24-35.

van der Kolk, B. A. (1988). The trauma spectrum: The interaction of biological and social events in the genesis of the trauma response. **Journal of Traumatic Stress, 1,** 273-290.

van der Kolk, B. A., & Saporta, J. (1991). The biological response to psychic trauma: Mechanisms and treatment of intrusion and numbing. **Anxiety Research, 4,** 199-212.

Van Houten, R. (1993). The use of wrist weights to reduce self-injury maintained by sensory reinforcement. **Journal of Applied Behavior Analysis, 26,** 197-204.

van Praag, H., Asnis, G. M., Kahn, R. S., Brown, S. L., Korn, M., Karkavy-Friedman, J. M., & Wetzler, S. (1990). Monoamines and abnormal behavior: A multiaminergic perspective. **British Journal of Psychiatry, 157,** 723-734.

Vitiello, B., Spreat, S., & Behar, D. (1989). Obsessive-compulsive disorder in mentally retarded patients. **Journal of Nervous and Mental Disease, 177,** 232-236.

Vollmer, T. R., Iwata, B. A., Zarcone, J. R., Smith, R. G., & Mazaleski, J. L. (1993). The role of attention in the treatment of attention-maintained self-injurious behavior: Noncontingent reinforcement and differential reinforcement of other behavior. **Journal of Applied Behavior Analysis, 26,** 9-21.

Wacker, D. P., Steege, M. W., Northup, J., Sasso, G., Berg, W., Reimers, T., Cooper, L., Cigrand, K., & Donn, L. (1990). A component analysis of functional communication training across three topographies of severe behavior problems. **Journal of Applied Behavior Analysis, 23**, 417-429.

Watson, J., Singh, N. N., & Winton, A. S. (1986). Suppressive effects of visual and facial screening on self-injurious finger sucking. **American Journal of Mental Deficiency, 90**, 526-534.

Weeks, M. & Gaylord-Ross, R. (1981). Task difficulty and aberrant behavior in severely handicapped students. **Journal of Applied Behavior Analysis, 14**, 449-463.

Weiher, R. G., & Harman, R. E. (1975). The use of omission training to reduce self-injurious behavior in a retarded child. **Behavior Therapy, 6**, 261-268.

Welch, L., & Sovner, R. (1992). The treatment of chronic organic mental disorder with dextromethorphan in a man with severe mental retardation. **British Journal of Psychiatry, 161**, 118-120.

Wells, M. E., & Smith, D. W. (1983). Reduction of self-injurious behavior of mentally retarded persons using sensory-integrative techniques. **American Journal of Mental Deficiency, 87**, 664-666.

Whitman, T. L., Scibak, J. W., & Reid, D. H. (1983). **Behavior modification with the severely and profoundly retarded: Research and application**. New York: Academic Press.

Winchel, R. M., & Stanley, M. (1991). Self-injurious behavior: A review of the behavior and biology of self-mutilation. **American Journal of Psychiatry, 148**, 306-317.

Wise, M. G. (1987). Delirium. In R. E. Hales & S. C. Yudofsky (Eds.), **Textbook of neuropsychiatry** (pp 89-103). Washington, DC: American Psychiatric Press.

Wolf, M., Risley, T., Johnston, M., Harris, F., & Allen, E., (1967). Application of operant conditioning procedures to the behavior problems of an autistic child. A follow-up and extension. **Behavior Research and Therapy, 5,** 103-111.

Wolf, M., Risley, T., & Mees, H. (1964). Application of operant conditioning procedures to the behaviour problems of an autistic child. **Behaviour Research and Therapy, 1,** 305-312.

Zarcone, J. R., Iwata, B. A., Hughes, C. E., & Vollmer, T. R. (1993a). Momentum versus extinction effects in the treatment of self-injurious behavior. **Journal of Applied Behavior Analysis, 26,** 135-136.

Zarcone, J. R., Iwata, B. A., Vollner, T. R., Jagtiani, S., Smith, R. G., & Mazaleski, J. I. (1993b). Extinction of self-injurious escape behavior with and without instructional fading. **Journal of Applied Behavior Analysis, 26,** 353-360.

SUBJECT INDEX

TREATMENT MANUALS FOR PRACTITIONERS IN DEVELOPMENTAL DISABILITIES

William I. Gardner, Series Editor

SELF-INJURIOUS BEHAVIORS
William I. Gardner
Robert Sovner

Future Titles

ANXIETY AND MOOD DISORDERS
William I. Gardner
Janice L. Graeber

BEHAVIORAL AND EMOTIONAL DISORDERS:
A MULTIMODAL FUNCTIONAL APPROACH
William I. Gardner

COPING AND SELF-MANAGEMENT SKILLS TRAINING
William I. Gardner
Laura K. Brutting

DISRUPTIVE BEHAVIOR DISORDERS
William I. Gardner
Robert Sovner

EATING DISORDERS
ANOREXIA NERVOSA, PICA, RUMINATIVE VOMITING
William I. Gardner